Effective Schools:
Three Case Studies of Excellence.

by Robert S. Gilchrist

concluding chapter
by
Deede Sharpe

The Manuscript for
Effective Schools: Three Case Studies of Excellence
was prepared for publication under the technical supervision
of Ida Morris, Marysville, Tennessee

Cover designed by Charles Neumeyer

Printed in the United States of America

CONTENTS

Effective Schools: Three Case Studies of Excellence is one of many publications produced by the National Educational Service. Our mission is to provide you and other leaders in education, business and government with top quality publications, videos, and conferences. If you have any questions or comments about *Effective Schools: Three Case Studies of Excellence* or any of our other publications or services, please contact us at:

National Educational Service
1821 W. 3rd. St., Suite 201
P.O. Box 8
Bloomington, IN 47402
(812) 336-7700

PREFACE

If I have learned nothing else during my lifetime in education, it is that democracy can't survive without good schools and that schools are only as good as their communities make them. To put it another way: Our schools are much too important to be entrusted entirely to the professionals — citizens can and should take active roles in making their schools as good as the best in the nation.

The "best" in the nation? Who are these "best?" Who says they are the "best?" Who determines how they will be judged the "best?" What criteria will be used for measuring overall ratings? Is there some magic formula that schools can follow to ensure a "best" rating? These are some of the questions I wanted my book to answer. I also wanted to study how we got where we are and where we ought to go from here.

During my research, I was able to observe firsthand teachers and students as they worked together in three schools, two of which had been identified as excellent in the 1984 School Recognition Program of the U. S. Department of Education and its Commission on Excellence, and the other by the national honor society, Kappa Delta Pi. In the process, I discovered so many good things going on at these schools that I felt compelled to share my observations with citizens who are concerned about education, or the lack of it, in modern America.

At the same time, I was depressed by what I heard in conversations and read in the newspapers and saw on television about the state of education in America — things like: "In the 1950s and the 1960s, people cared about their schools. Now everyone is so busy making money that they can't be bothered." This from a citizen who had been a school board member for many years.

Another time a school principal told me of his meeting with a journalist sent to gather information for his newspaper following the vandalization of the school. When the reporter had exhausted questions regarding estimated damages and possible identity of the culprits, the principal asked him if he

1

would like to see some of the science projects just finished by students at the school. The reporter was quick to respond, "No, thanks. People want to hear about what's wrong with their schools — positive stories don't seem to interest them."

Because of comments such as these, I became aware that the media — newspapers, radio, TV and magazines — were giving schools a bad name. They seldom report what's going on in good schools. In the name of objectivity, I suppose, most media exposure stops short of analyzing why schools have problems. Often, the impression lingers that the schools are at fault — not the changes in society that have brought new problems to the schools. No one was saying what I thought concerned citizens should hear and what my experience has taught me: that a school can make good only when its staff is committed to making it the best, and to do this they must have the help and support of parents and the community.

National pronouncements about the decline of our schools and what we should do to improve them, along with news of laws being passed by state legislatures requiring more academic subjects and longer school hours, were telling only part of the story. Assumptions seemed to be that adding one more year of a required subject such as English would automatically improve reading and writing abilities of the students. To many people, the release of a report of a national commission on education was tantamount to its recommendations being put into action.

From January, 1982, until November, 1985, I coordinated the Grandpeople Program, first at Westwood Elementary School and then at Twin Peaks Middle School in the Poway Unified School District in California. The schools already had volunteer programs for their parents, but this Grandpeople Program was unique in that it gave the citizens who did not have children in school an opportunity not only to help the school, but also to learn firsthand about the program of the school — how good or bad it was.

From the first day I began my volunteer job as coordinator of the Grandpeople Program at Twin Peaks, described later in detail, I knew there was something different about this particular school. The school climate was warm and friendly, flowing from the administration through the teachers and on to the students. Students appeared to enjoy the serious side of their classwork as much as the fun side of school, through its wide range of extracurricular activities.

Working in these schools half-time gave me a wonderful opportunity to get acquainted with the staffs and programs which were being offered to the students. I found that most of the teachers were literally "knocking themselves out" to provide high quality experiences for their students. They made my job of matchmaking a challenge. They told me their needs, and I found citizens whose abilities and past experiences enabled them to fill the needs.

2

In the summer of 1984, Twin Peaks was recognized nationally as being one of the most outstanding 88 middle and junior high schools throughout the United States. I began to ponder why all of our schools couldn't be as good as our best schools, and what our best schools actually do to become outstanding.

My first step in finding answers to questions like these was to learn more about the secondary school recognition program which began in the school year 1982-1983 under the leadership of Secretary of Education, Dr. Terrel Bell. Dr. Bell started the project as a follow-up of the work of the Commission on Excellence in Education which produced the book, *A Nation at Risk*.

The selection process is a very comprehensive procedure. The Department of Education in Washington, D. C., first asks each state's Department of Education to nominate outstanding schools, who in turn ask county Departments of Education to identify outstanding schools in their counties. Schools selected by the county office as eligible for consideration are then invited to apply by providing data on criteria used for selection. These attributes numbered fourteen: Goals, Expectations, Discipline, Rewards, Monitoring, Responsiblity, Teacher Efficacy, Incentives, A.L.T. (Academic Learning Time), Positive Climate, Leadership, Articulation, Evaluation, and Community Support.

The completed applications from each county are screened by the state's Department of Education. The state department then sends the applications which have been considered most outstanding to Washington, D. C. The number of final applications each state can submit is pre-determined.

In San Diego County, the selection process began when the county's Department of Education was asked to nominate ten outstanding high schools and middle schools from its district. Completed applications from each of the ten San Diego County schools, as well as several hundred others from throughout California, were initially screened by the state's Department of Education. Of these, eighteen California schools stood out as "outstanding," and their applications progressed to Washington, D. C. for additional in-depth judgment.

From around the country emerged a total of 550 schools to be examined by a federal review panel, which included on-site visits. Panel members consisted of principals, teachers, superintendents and state and national school board members. Also active on the panel were high-ranking business and foundation representatives, as well as a former state governor. These reviewers then reported their findings to the U. S. Department of Education High School Panel and the National Commission on Excellence in Education.

Finally, after careful screening, 202 secondary public schools and 60 private schools were selected as exemplary at the national level, with Twin Peaks as one of them. The Twin Peaks formal recognition ceremony back in Poway, California, was an occasion long to be remembered by the entire school.

McCluer North High School, in the Ferguson-Florissant School District in St. Louis County, Missouri, received the award the same year as Twin Peaks received theirs. I had already heard many positive comments about the advisory program at McCluer North and also the very effective way in which the school had followed through on the court desegregation order. I was eager to learn exactly how McCluer North, an integrated, urban high school, had achieved excellence.

The U. S. Department of Education did not have a recognition program for elementary schools in 1984, so I turned to Kappa Delta Pi, an honor society in education, to help me find an outstanding elementary school in the South that I could focus my studies on.

In 1981, Kappa Delta Pi had launched a Good Schools Project, resulting in publication in 1984 of the book, *One Hundred Good Schools*. I asked Dr. Jack Frymier of Ohio State University, who directed the project, to nominate an outstanding elementary school that I could visit. After conferring with Kappa Delta Pi officers, Dr. Frymier nominated Garden Hills Elementary School in Atlanta, Georgia. The National Recognition Program began including elementary schools in 1985-1986, when Garden Hills was also designated as an excellent school.

Now that I had a clear picture of the steps involved in the selection procedure, I was eager to learn as much as I could about how each of these schools was able to excel and others not. Although much was publicized about laudable school practices, very little space, if any, was given to how each school went about planning and implementing them; and if other schools were to benefit from their examples, they would have to know the "how" as well as the "what." I wanted to find out what was happening in the classrooms and on campus. I wanted to be where the action was — where students met staff members, where learning took place, and I would begin at Twin Peaks Middle School.

This, then, would be my objective, with the consent and cooperation of the Twin Peaks principal and staff, and in addition to my part-time role at the school as "Grandpeople" coordinator: I would devote as much time as necessary to learn all I could about how this school's operation resulted in its national recognition for excellence.

I attended faculty meetings. As a silent observer, I visited at least three classes in each subject field. I became a spectator at many on- and off-campus activities. I sat in on student council meetings and student court sessions. I went to classes for the entire day with students in grades six, seven and eight. I attended School Site Committee meetings which included staff, students and parents. I interviewed teachers and students, privately and collectively, seeking opinions about their school — its pluses and minuses.

4

Having thus completed my study of Twin Peaks and reached what I thought were unshakeable conclusions, I would not rest until I could confirm them with additional research. I had to know if different factors influence the quality of education at different grade levels. Are other forces at work which produce superior elementary or high schools? The only way I would find out would be to spend equal time at those kinds of schools and see if, indeed, they shared common denominators.

In the fall of 1985, I visited McCluer North High School for five weeks, and then went on to Garden Hills Elementary School in January, 1986, and spent another five weeks there. At McCluer North, I also visited classes as a silent observer, talked with students, became a spectator at many on- and off-campus activities, sat in on student council and other student committees. I went to classes with a student at each grade level for a full day. At Garden Hills I spoke with all the teachers in individual conferences, attended all faculty meetings and PTA meetings and visited with the children.

After completing my initial visits at the three schools and following them up with return trips to verify certain data — a lengthy process that included input from principals at each school, staff members, students, parents and others — several dominant findings became clear:

Excellent schools, from grade one through twelve, cannot be attained without a committed staff and help and support of parents and community;

Practices that have been found to be successful in one school do not always produce the same results in another school; and

Successful schools have similar characteristics, elements in common, that provide the basis for their superiority.

Effective Schools: Three Case Studies of Excellence was documented to bring readers up to date on what is happening in three excellent schools. Its purpose is to detail the methods by which these schools achieved recognition, and to offer suggestions to concerned citizens who want to help make their schools better but don't know where to begin.

R. S. G.

5

ACKNOWLEDGEMENTS

If it were not for the staff, students, parents and community citizens of three schools, my editors, advisors, contributing author and my family, this book never would have been written.

Learning to know the three schools was exciting. Judy Endeman at Twin Peaks, Bill Hampton at McCluer North and Peggy Geren at Garden Hills, principals of the three schools, insisted that their doors were open to me whenever I needed more information. The degree of cooperation I received was outstanding. For example, one morning at 10, I asked Dr. Geren how I could get more background on how the school had been able to obtain a room full of computers. That same day, so I could get the information I wanted as quickly as possible, a lengthy luncheon was arranged with the involved Atlanta computer distributor who could answer all my questions.

Without the help of the teachers, I never could have learned how the schools developed many of their excellent practices. Teachers not only took the time to confer with me about what individual members had done in strengthening the learning programs, but also arranged my contacts with entire classrooms or individual students.

At McCluer North I was eager to learn what teachers thought of the school's advisory program, especially since changes outside the school and within the student body raised many questions about how the advisory program should be organized. Three advisors, Kathleen Dombrink, Neta Pope and Douglas Lane, each committed to the soundness of the advisory program, placed conferences with me on their priority lists.

At Garden Hills the basic room teachers worked hard to be sure that all the basic subjects were given adequate attention during the time the students were in the basic classroom and not out of the room for computer, physical education and other offerings. Elizabeth Etheridge, second grade teacher, took the time to make a chart to clarify the problem for me.

A common thread runs through the staffs of the three schools: pride in their accomplishments is accompanied with humility in the realization that there is still much to be done, especially since everything outside the schools is changing so fast. These elements of pride and humility help explain why these schools are recognized as outstanding.

I am grateful to the students of these schools for renewing and deepening my faith in youth. I especially appreciate the help of the 8th grade boy who wrote up for me how the "Indianapolis 500" Spirit Day event started and who did the work to make it a success. I asked him to do this as I watched the race one day. He brought his story to me the very next day.

When I had tapes to transcribe, the typing teacher recommended a student who had taken typing as an elective for only six months. The student said she would be glad to do the typing and needed convincing to accept payment for her night and weekend typing efforts.

I felt confident after my research was completed that these three schools were fulfilling their mission. Most of the students with whom I came in contact were visible proof that they were profiting from their schooling. Without cooperations from the students, I could not have arrived at this conclusion.

Parents and other community citizens helped me to write the chapter devoted to volunteers. Also, during my work with Twin Peaks and while visiting McCluer North and Garden Hills, I supplemented discussions and attendance at scheduled meetings with telephone calls and conferences with interested lay people. Their quotations and comments reflected an unrehearsed sincerity, and I wish to acknowledge my deep gratitude to these people for their contributions to this book.

I am indebted to editors Ida Morris and Ben Brodinsky, who painstakingly revised my original drafts into a continuity of readable paragraphs and chapters. Mrs. Morris and I have worked together on many writing projects spanning 25 years — and, considering the legibility of my handwriting, it is a miracle that we are even still speaking! Mr. Brodinsky, because of his experience as editor-in-chief of Croft Educational Services, is much in demand to edit publications of major organizations, like AASA (American Association of School Administrators). Despite his crowded schedule, however, he accepted my invitation to participate in many editorial decisions required in this book.

I saw my role in producing this book primarily as a journalist reporting the news of three schools. I petitioned Deede Sharpe, formerly of Walt Disney World Co. and now a consultant working with forward-looking schools, to contribute the wrap-up chapter, "Seven Common Characteristics of Good Schools and What We Can Learn from Them." The intent of this chapter is to identify basic human principles as they are applied in the world of business and to show how Garden Hills, Twin Peaks and McCluer North schools rely on these same principles to guide them toward excellence. The author then suggests ways for readers to help improve their schools.

I work and produce best when I have the benefit of ideas of colleagues whom I respect — not "yes" people, but individuals who have ideas of their own. After weighing various viewpoints, I then arrive at my own decisions, incorporating or rejecting the ideas of others. I couldn't possibly record the names of all the people who helped me during the researching, writing and editing of this book; it would require another volume.

Those who come to mind immediately, however, include Tony Bechtold, Bruce Braciszewski, Derek Burleson, George Brain, Ron Brandt, Doreen Dumas, William deYoung, William Dick, Walter Fisher, Jack Frymier, Ann Guinn, Don Hair, Katie Hart, Marie Hawk, Louis Hodig, Suejean Jeffries, Sharon Kane, Richard Keeton, Irvin Levey, Alvin Marks, Gary Marx, Patrick Mitchell, Carl Nelson, Lincoln Parker, Sandy Pasqua, Susie Pearce, Patricia Peyton, John Pletcher, Leona Plummer, Renee and Dean Rasmussen, Mary Rauch, Linda Rayburn, John Richardson, Maureen Robertson, Phyllis Savon, Scribbler's Club of Rancho Bernardo, Thomas Sergiovanni, Harold Shane, Art Shostach, Michael Thacker, David Turney, Glenys Unruh, William Van Til, Norman Watson and Charles Welch. I am certain that I have overlooked many — please accept my apology.

Working on this book for three and a half years has obviously disrupted family life. I owe Adele, my wife, a special note of gratitude. She not only adjusted to my schedule of research and writing, but also actively became an enthusiastic partner on our travels to visit the two schools in St. Louis and Atlanta. She also helped by reacting to my ideas as I moved along in planning.

Our relatives and close friends deserve thanks, too. In our visits, either in our home or theirs, I am sure that I did not hide very well my preoccupation and sometimes my worry with the book. This would apply especially to our three, now grown children, Lou, William and Suzy. I am assuring them that I now hope to return to normalcy.

R. S. G.

CHAPTER ONE

The Long Road Upward — from the one-room school to the school of today

Through these pages the reader will enter a world of schools and education which would have mystified Socrates, amazed Rousseau, and boggled the minds of Pestalozzi and even Montessori. These great educators of the past (and others, too) might possibly have sensed the love and respect for human individuality that permeates today's education. But they probably would also have been overwhelmed by the great variety of students our schools serve today, by the richness of modern course offerings, and by the almost awesome physical environments provided by many of our present day schools.

They would hardly grasp the theories and concepts which dominate learning and teaching today; and would undoubtedly have found incomprehensible today's school practices known by such labels as audio-visual programs, microfiche, computer literacy, curriculum revision, school food services, guidance and staff development.

The teaching and learning taking place today in our best schools, such as those described in this book, might have been equally incomprehensible even to our grandparents and parents.

To comprehend in all its enormity the strides education has made even in the last sixty-plus years, we could begin by refreshing our memories about what school life was like in the 1920s when I first began to teach. My personal memories do not cover the schools of such big cities as Boston, Philadelphia, St. Louis or Cincinnati. But they do cover schooling as it was practiced in more than 90 percent of American communities, which were largely rural or just becoming urbanized.

Textbooks contained what students should learn, and teachers found out how well students had learned through recitation, oral and written quizzes. Learning was primarily by rote. Science classes emphasized the retention of facts and figures, not the concepts of the scientific process. Quiet seatwork was thought to be a cardinal virtue in the classroom.

In the typical rural and small town school of that day, architectural design was certainly not a prime factor, and "convenience" in any form was overshadowed by "necessity" or "survival" — hence, the usefulness of the one-room schoolhouse. One school served a number of farm families separated by long distances, and just getting to school for many students was a daily challenge. Ventilation was poor because protection from the cold during the winter was considered more important than keeping cool; a wood-burning pot-bellied stove, tended by one of the boys, kept the classes warm during the cold weather.

In those days a person didn't have to be too educated to teach school. Teachers were often slightly older than some of their students and had a minimum of teacher training. Lack of teacher training, however, was often overcome by intense dedication and commitment.

In the 1920s, Colorado and other states certified teachers for employment in rural and small town elementary schools on two conditions: if they had graduated from high school, and if they could pass tests in each of the subject fields that made up the programs in elementary schools.

Two months after graduating from high school in June, 1922, I took and passed the teacher's exam. During 1922-1923, I taught 5th grade at an 8-teacher rural school in the sugar beet and potato country, in the town of Severance, between Greeley and Fort Collins, Colorado. My salary was $1,000 a year. My preparation for teaching, I must confess, was meager at best: I taught as I was taught. I did take a course on teaching methods during my junior year in high school and one summer school session at Colorado Teachers College (now Northern Colorado University) at Greeley. It's safe to say that similar limited preparation was common for teachers in many regions throughout the United States during the 1920s and the 1930s.

Who attended school at Severance was usually decided on the basis of whether or not it was physically possible to reach the school and what needed most to be done at home or on the farm. The older the students became — and this was mostly true of boys — the more frequent their absences from school. Farm chores or harvest times required the help of strong, young bodies — school could be postponed, but the chores of survival couldn't wait. The number of years of schooling was tied closely to conditions on the farm, or early marriage, with schooling through grade 8 being the norm.

I recall that at Severance, school was dismissed for a week at the height of the potato harvest in the fall, and I joined members of my class and their parents in this essential farm activity. Eight to ten people would each take a half-bushel basket and put into them the potatoes that had been brought to the surface of the ground by machinery. We tried desperately to keep up with the wagon into which we dumped our heavy baskets.

In 1923-1924, I was principal and taught grades 5 through 9 high in the Rockies at Pitkin, Colorado. Despite frequent 20-degree below weather which confined us to one room for the entire day, austerity of environment and scarcity of resources, school was rarely dull or unchallenging. A typical school day went something like this: While I worked with four 9th graders in algebra, students in other grades worked at their desks on other subjects. What we now call "peer teaching" was a common practice — for instance, a 6th grade student would work with any students with their spelling. Rote memorization was the normal routine. At 11:30 every morning, a 5th grade girl would put a kettle of soup on the stove so we could have something hot as part of our lunch.

Recess and noon period provided time for relaxation and fun. Tumbling on mattresses that had been donated by parents and placed in the aisles was a favorite activity. Friday, after recess, if we'd done our work well, we'd have a spelling contest. Planning with students at recess time, chatting with individuals at the end of the day, and visiting some of them at their homes, I learned to know the students and they learned to know me.

We had no provision for industrial arts or home economics courses, but the students found ways to make up for the deficiency. On one occasion, when they expressed a desire to construct an exhibit for the County Fair, I said, "But we have no place to do that." They said, "We'll find a place," and they did — the coal house at the back of the two-story schoolhouse. I said, "But I don't know anything about carpentry," and they said, "We'll get our fathers to help us on Saturdays, and we can use their tools." The girls said, "We want to enter the sewing competition." I said, "But we have no sewing machines and no sewing teacher," and they said, "We'll find someone who can teach us, and we can use our mothers' machines," and they did. And they earned a blue ribbon at the fair.

After securing my bachelor's and master's degrees in math and education at Colorado Teachers college in 1928, I worked as a principal in three different junior high schools before 1935 when I became principal of Greeley High School in Greeley, Colorado. In the 1930s, I earned around $3,600 a year.

The activities program at Greeley High School was considered unique when compared to the 1935 norm at other schools. The lunch period consisted of an hour-and-a-half, which now seems like a long time, but inasmuch as we were still in the throes of the Depression and cars were not available, many students walked home for lunch. In time available for students who remained at the school, they played softball, read in the library, danced in the gym or took part in a club activity. During the last half-hour of the lunch period teachers were in their classrooms, making themselves available to students who wanted to confer with them privately.

11

What we now refer to as "staff development" — that is, the upgrading of teachers on the job — was in a rudimentary stage. Greeley teachers enrolled in courses leading toward advanced degrees, or went to state and national conferences to pick up new facts and ideas about their subject matter fields. They were then encouraged to share what they had learned with the rest of the faculty.

As for teacher recognition, an important factor today in raising teacher morale, that can best be summed up as "You were either in or you were out." Since there was little opportunity for interaction with teachers in other schools, due to the restrictions of money, space and travel, there was no opportunity for being singled out — unless, of course, you didn't do your job well, and then you were "out."

Today, deciding what children should learn involves a complex process of curriculum development. Years ago it used to be quite simple to develop — to take one example — a social studies program. Children first learned about their homes and immediate neighborhoods. From there they learned about their community where the fire department, police force, and other "helpers" became their friends. By the time students got to high school, they had studied a bit of United States history and possibly some European and then world history. What a nice developmental sequence, or so it seemed.

Nearly all social studies programs of the 1940s touched on the life and work of Franklin Delano Roosevelt who instituted innovative national initiatives to combat the monumental unemployment and other ravages of the Depression. (Interestingly, Garden Hills Elementary School in Atlanta, Georgia, was constructed as the result of one of F. D. R.'s programs to put men to work — the WPA, or the Works Progress Administration.) But the social studies of only a few decades ago ignored major segments of information: the contribution of blacks and the development of countries in the Orient, to name but two.

Middle years of the 20th Century provide dramatic evidence that what happens in society profoundly affects our schools. The G. I. Bill of Rights, for example, passed in 1944, irreversibly altered our thinking about who should go to school. The law provided, among other benefits, money for tuition, counseling and job placement for millions of World War II veterans. The G. I. Bill not only affirmed the reality that adults can learn at any age and should continue to learn all their lives — it also emphasized the importance and value of education for all classes of society. I regard the G. I. bill as the forerunner of a new kind of thinking in America — one that says that all adults should be learning all of their lives because conditions change so fast that old skills and understandings will no longer sustain them throughout life.

Early English courses emphasized diagramming and parsing (separating a sentence into parts). When students read "The Lady and the Lake," the purpose was to analyze the content and the life of the author. Teachers did not help us understand the basic reason for taking English. It was not until a generation later that we discovered the real reason for taking English: to learn to speak, write and read effectively, and to enjoy literature.

The way we taught science and math underwent a severe shakeup when the Soviet satellite, Sputnik, was launched in 1957. The world of education was blamed for not having produced top-notch scientists to beat the Soviets into space. Congress hurried to enact the National Defense Education Act to try to catch up. Money was made available for teacher education, materials, and equipment. Later, President Kennedy led the nation in a successful effort to outdo the Soviets, and we moved quickly to advance our space program, enabling us to be the first to put a man on the moon.

Still another national event was to affect the way schools operated. Following the death of President John F. Kennedy, and after being elected to a full term, Lyndon B. Johnson worked to correct civil rights inequities. His war-on-poverty legislation contained the condition that advisory committees would be required for any school projects on which federal money was being used; and in the case of school funding, advisory committees had to include as many parents as staff members. In effect, this legislation laid the foundation for the expanding role that parents (who had up until now been largely ignored) began to play in the operation of their schools.

As more people were able to participate in higher education, more began to look down their noses at students enrolled in vocational courses, until one day we woke up to discover there was a shortage of skilled labor. Here was a costly lesson, and we are only now returning to some degree of reality about the dire need for vocational training. The truth has sunk in that academic educatoin is not for everyone, and some schools are now trying to make corrections which will successfully balance the right blend of academics and vocational studies.

In 1954, another major social change took place as a result of the Supreme Court's decision in the landmark case of Brown vs. the Board of Education of Topeka, one that opened even further the doors of the nation's schools to anyone and everyone. The excellent schools described in this book illustrate some ways in which we have capitalized on racial and cultural differences to make learning beneficial for large segments of society.

During the Eisenhower administration (1952-1960), a new national network of highways added impetus to the communication and transportation explosion already created by the advent of television and aviation advances. We began to learn more about the world, and we began to learn it much earlier in life through our exposure to television. These changes forced us to devise strategies for enlarging the learning process and for learning from persons whose region, culture, and lifestyle differ from ours.

We now find ourselves in a world totally different from the one we left behind. Between 1920 and 1988, U. S. population has more than doubled.

Far more people live in large urban areas than in small towns. The number of pupils in rural school districts compose only a fraction of the number in the early part of the century.

Schools today operate the largest bus transportation business in the country largely because students are transported to schools out of their home districts to achieve better balance between blacks and whites, and because it's not safe for students to walk on a highway. We live in a world of fast cars, microwave ovens and power stations, television, electronic pianos, copy machines, fluorescent lights, credit cards, ball-point pens, icemakers, video cassette recorders, dishwashers, clothes driers, electric blankets, pizza pies, instant coffee. Global and national changes have affected us socially and economically, and they have also altered the entire educational process.

Our school buildings have been transformed, in many instances, into modern, efficient plants designed to enhance student learning. Administrators and teachers have been prepared for their responsibilities in our better teacher education institutions. Education through high school is available for all youth, and schools are challenged to provide appropriate programs for all youth.

Along the way we've discovered a lot about the way people learn and about human development in general. We've found, for instance, that although students learn some things well in large groups, classes can also be divided into small groups to concentrate on sharpening special skills or mastering new subject matter. We've also discovered the importance of giving students individual attention and encouraging them to work independently.

The importance of developing a student's self-esteem and self-worth has been established by research, and experts now believe that program offerings should enable each student to succeed if he or she works hard. The powerful role of motivation is also agreed upon as important, for research has found that skills will be retained longer and used more effectively outside the classroom if students see meaning in what they are doing. Read how each of the three schools described in this book infuse the learning environment with meaning and challenge for their students.

Some subjects that students study today may have the same names, but the content and method of presentation are different, due in no small measure to the permeation of television into our lives. Social studies, mentioned earlier, have undergone numerous changes. We no longer rely on the old way of presenting history, for children in their living rooms have become acquainted with the whole world as soon as they're able to watch and understand what the big screen shows.

Later in this book we learn how Twin Peaks Middle School meets head on the old problem of how to stimulate young people to read more. For one thing, discerning teachers in that school and parents have agreed that students will develop into better readers when they are encouraged to read on school time an interesting book at their own reading level.

A marvelous range of instructional material is now available to teachers, including audio-visual resources, maps, microfilm, periodicals, graphics, and a wide variety of pamphlets and booklets published by organizations in every field of endeavor.

We no longer have to rely on tumbling on mattresses in classroom aisles as an extra-curricular activity; today's schools offer a rich menu from which students can select activities for the sheer joy of expanding their interests and skills. All of the schools described in forthcoming chapters offer their students a stimulating and exciting array of activities, many of which are spurred on by parent and community participation.

Efforts to keep up with latest developments in education dictate that teachers (and administrators) never stop exploring new ideas and methods through travel, conferences, seminars, community interaction and membership in professional organizations. Close to 1,000 national, regional, state and local associations — devoted to every conceivable subject, from art to science to physical education — function to advance the knowledge, methods and materials teachers and administrators need for their daily operation.

Citizens and community leaders are assuming more ownership in their schools either as individual volunteers or through their places of business. Astute business people, recognizing the school's potential to provide them with well-educated, well-adjusted employees, are increasingly forming partnerships with the school. Some large companies cooperate by providing summer jobs for students and guaranteeing employment following high school or college graduation. An example is the Boston Compact Program which involves schools, businesses and universities in the Boston area.

The concept of recognizing schools or individual teachers for exceptional performance is relatively new. The process is most meaningful for both schools and teachers when it is conducted regularly in order to evaluate progress or lack of it, and to point the way to improvement where needed. Being judged outstanding by one's peers brings with it an inspiring morale-boosting reward for having done an excellent job and a challenge to do better.

The pages that follow present two reasonable conclusions why Garden Hills, Twin Peaks, and McCluer North made good: They tried hard to profit from the past, and they tried hard to keep up to date. The final hurdle that put them over the top (and one that every school must ultimately address) was the manner in which they prepared for the future.

But what, after all, can we predict about our future?

We know that we will all live longer, healthier lives, doing more things that give us pleasure than things we consider "hard work." We know also that not too far in the future lies the dire prospect of having more people on earth than we can feed or house. We know that when President Truman made the decision to drop the atom bomb on Hiroshima, the entire world changed, to be ever fearful of an even more terrifying holocaust capable of destroying civilization and all forms of life.

And if we didn't already sense it, Distinguished Rank Professor of Indiana University's School of Education, Harold G. Shane, reminds us that we are moving toward an information glut — a run-away race that will double our rate of information every two years beginning in 1992. Since no one can retain even a tiny fraction of the information that is available and important to us, Professor Shane tells us, we will have to find new ways to select and analyze information rather than merely acquire it.

He recommends that we develop what he calls "anticipatory hindsight" — or, the ability to anticipate future needs while at the same time benefiting from the past in order to avoid past errors.

Shane says this means that "our schools must become creative learning centers, serving persons of all ages rather than merely functioning in the role of repositories of information from times past."

Perhaps the most critical question of all is, When and where do children get an education?

The three schools described in this book believe that a child learns whenever he or she is awake.

This means that the home, school and community, ideally, should be working together to decide how each can develop the best possible environment for the growth and development of our youth. The home should see to it that a child's needs, such as nutrition, sleep, feelings of security and self respect, and a balance in kinds of activities, are met. And, in turn, the schools have the obligation to lead in providing for development in reading, writing, mathematics, thinking, problem-solving and understanding our country and the world.

If a school can reach an understanding about the role it shares with the home and community in developing a young person's education, the school will be able to do its job better. This is what happened at Garden Hills, Twin Peaks and McCluer North schools.

It can happen at your school, too.

CHAPTER TWO

Garden Hills Elementary School: A School That Throbs with Life and Learning

1.

At 7:30 in the morning, one late December day, I headed for Garden Hills Elementary School from downtown Atlanta. Travelling north on Peachtree Road, I reached the Buckhead section of north Atlanta. As I left downtown the buildings became more varied. First, I passed a conglomerate of retail businesses, commercial and professional offices, churches, motels, foreign consulates; then the beginnings of a residential area emerged. Next, I passed the Peachtree Battle Shopping Mall. Further on I observed a high-rise condominium under construction with hundreds of "hard-hats" on the job, adding another story to the already 34-story structure. Turning right onto Sheridan Drive, I passed through a large wooded park which led to a wide open expanse and a children's playground. Then, to the east of this area loomed a stately two-story brick building, its front door framed by massive white pillars, in the traditional Southern mansion manner. Garden Hills School was before me.

Garden Hills is a kindergarten through fifth grade elementary school. My visit, which stretched into about five weeks, was prompted because of its recognition as a superior, multi-racial elementary school. In 1985-86 its enrollment was 380 — 33 percent black, 32 percent white (American, European and Middle East), 21 percent Asian (including the Pacific Isles), and 14 percent Hispanic — a blend of pupils who came from 34 countries and spoke 21 different languages.

The scholastic achievement of these students was impressive. California Achievement Tests, designed to measure basic skills, show that in 1985 Garden Hills students scored at what educators call the 94th percentile. Inasmuch as the 50th percentile is considered the median score of all the pupils who take standardized achievement tests throughout the nation, it is easy to see why Garden Hills qualified as an outstanding school.

Just before I opened the door, I noticed an engraving on the building, saying that it had been constructed in 1937 by the Works Progress Administration. Once inside and to the left, it was not hard to spot the general office — it was the area humming with sounds resulting from a never-ending procession of students, teachers and parents. To its left was the principal's office which, as I learned later, is seldom occupied. The principal is usually out among the classrooms, observing or meeting with individual teachers or groups.

An easel in the front corridor displayed a placard reading "Garden Hills — an International School" which was highlighted by an arrangement of small flags of many nations. At still another level, just before the gymnasium entrance, I saw evidence of the holiday season. A large fir tree sparkled with lights, and the theme of universality revealed itself again through the tree's ornaments which were student-made paper dolls colorfully adorned in native costumes.

As I walked through the corridors, I noticed other displays of student and teacher creativity, all of which held out the promise that this old building was not only a comfortable place, but a pleasant place as well, to live, work and study.

I am not alone in my initial assessment of what I saw that first day. Later, during my five-week stay, one of the new teachers told me that the minute she walked into Garden Hills for an interview she knew that this was the school for her. When I asked her why she chose this school over two other job possibilities, she said, "It's hard to explain, but there is something in the air here that makes you feel good."

With my initiation day behind me, I looked forward to "starting school" the next day — to find out what, besides its air, made this school one of the best in the country.

Eight big yellow buses arrive at the school entrance at approximately 7:45 in the morning, each school day. Many of the black boys and girls have ridden long distances from throughout the city to get here. They are pupils whose parents elect to send them to Garden Hills, out of their own districts, to achieve better integration. Those pupils who live within the Garden Hills school boundaries ride the same buses.

Upon entering the building, about half of the students go to the cafeteria for breakfast. Many participate in a federally funded breakfast program for low income families, while others have breakfast at the school as a convenience. The rest go to the gymnasium where they wait until 8:15 when school begins and then all of the pupils disperse to what are known as their "basic classrooms." "Basic" teachers have the same pupils for most of the day, with responsibilities for teaching language arts (reading, writing, speech and literature), math, social studies (history, geography and civics), science and art.

While most subjects are taught in the basic classrooms, pupils do go to other rooms at different times during the week for instruction in use of the computer, library skills or physical education. Two days a week a music teacher comes to the basic classroom to conduct music lessons, although music is often taught in the gymnasium-auditorium.

At other times certain students leave their basic rooms to participate in the state program for gifted children called "Challenge," or to go to a special education teacher for help in overcoming language difficulties. One-third of the students are in English as a Second Language (ESL) classes at some time during the day.

The halls at Garden Hills never seem empty. Besides the usual traffic created by boys and girls moving into and out of classrooms, washrooms, library, computer room, main office or cafeteria, small clusters of students gather in the halls, engrossed in group planning for a particular class or project. Because the cafeteria is small, lunch periods are staggered, requiring about two hours each day to complete the feeding cycle for all students. In spite of the heavy traffic, students seem orderly. They are not loitering — they know where they are going. However, the halls are empty between 9 a.m. and 10:30 a.m., the time reserved in all classrooms for intensive, uninterrupted concentration in reading and math skills. Both the teachers and pupils seem to appreciate this regulation and do not violate it.

The end of the school day is signalled by Principal Dr. Peggy Geren when, around 2:50 p.m., she uses the public address system to tell the pupils that it's time to get ready to go home. She bids them goodbye, wishes everyone a safe journey, warns about traffic hazards, and assures them the staff will be glad to see them again in the morning.

The students are gone, but teachers and other staff members remain. After school is the time for planning, conferences, and faculty meetings. After the children leave on Tuesday, for example, the entire staff meets for an hour or more to take up topics and questions about teaching, curriculum, and student problems. Wednesday, after school, is set aside for conferences with parents. Monday, Thursday and Friday staff members either meet in small groups or individual teachers work on whatever tops their priority list.

Teachers also utilize other available time to plan, while students are at breakfast or lunch or in the gym before school starts in the morning. Planning and preparation for carrying out the plans cannot always be done on school time — which is why I frequently noticed teachers carrying bulging brief cases as they left school for the day. In addition, the Atlanta school system provides five days for staff planning at the beginning of each school year and four days throughout the year.

But student programs and staff development did not always proceed harmoniously and on-course at Garden Hills. Early in 1979 Mr. Theo Vocales, who had been the school's principal for eleven years, retired and a new principal was hired during the summer. The appointment, however, was ill-fated; and for a variety of reasons it became necessary to dismiss the new principal after only a month on the job, leaving Garden Hills to begin a new school year without a leader.

The fall of 1979 found both the school and the community in a state of shock. Getting a school off to a good start at the beginning of any new term is difficult at best, but when it must be managed in an atmosphere of administrative upheaval, the task becomes especially complicated. Fortunately, the school successfully weathered the storm with the temporary return of its former principal, Mr. Vocales, and the exceptional help of staff members.

Dr. Peggy Geren was appointed principal of Garden Hills School late in 1979 by superintendent Dr. Alonzo Crim. Because of her extensive studies in the area of integration, Dr. Crim judged she would be good medicine for the beleaguered school. This was the decade of desegregation throughout the Atlanta schools, and in 1970 Dr. Geren, along with other Atlanta staff members, had received a year's leave of absence to study potential problems related to change-overs from segregation to integration. After reviewing Dr. Geren's credentials, many neighborhood parents agreed that she could provide the kind of leadership their school needed and seconded the appointment.

Previously Dr. Geren had served as principal for 12 years at a predominantly black school in Atlanta, an experience that prepared her well for her new position.

Peggy Geren welcomed this new opportunity, confident in her belief that children of various races and nationalities need to live and learn together if American ideals are to be preserved. Dr. Geren was helped by a nucleus of veteran teachers who were eager to go to work with her on the school's many problems. Four of these teachers, who were black, had been at Garden Hills for 10 or 11 years, arriving at the time staff desegregation was adopted and implemented in Atlanta schools in 1970. During the years 1978-1980 another black and three white teachers were employed, and it was this core of longtime staff members that would provide teacher-level leadership in planning and implementing school programs.

From the first day Principal Geren arrived at the school in January, 1980, she became engrossed in the pressing problems of Garden Hills — and there were many. She never stayed in one place in the school for very long. Even today Peggy Geren is generally hard to find and rarely in her office more than a tenth of the time between 7:30 a.m. (when the buses arrive) and 3:00 p.m. (when they leave).

Her school days are filled with tasks that take her to numerous locations throughout the building. She may be found in the main office, comforting a child who is sick and reassuring the youngster that a parent will be there soon or giving advice to a teacher who needs help with a discipline problem.

Sometimes she is called to the Regional III office, outside of the school. (The Atlanta system is divided into three areas, each with an associate superintendent in charge.) And much of her time is spent working with parent or community groups when she feels that her presence as captain or coordinator, can promote the interests of the school.

2.

Garden Hills operates according to the accepted business management premise that if any institution is to succeed, it must first draw up a blueprint — a plan that details a specific goal, philosophy, mission or commitment. Garden Hills' philosophy and mission have been stated as follows:

"We feel that the mission of the school is to have each child experience success in learning up to his or her potential."

"We feel that each student has unique educational needs, and that the child, teachers, parents and community should work together to identify and establish curriculum to meet the needs."

"We support the development of behaviors reflecting honesty, commitment, self-direction and responsibility. We feel that the school does a disservice if it emphasizes academic achievement and fails to teach responsible behavior."

"We feel that the school should prepare students for global citizenship. They should be able to perform as members of the family of mankind by showing responsibility and caring for people of cultures different from their own, acting as stewards of the earth and its resources and practicing the skills needed to resolve differences by peaceful means."

These statements of the school's philosophy are not merely an academic exercise — they are a declaration of the understandings which guide the staff and parents in their day-by-day, week-by-week and year-by-year work. Teachers discuss these statements with the students, and PTA leaders discuss them at PTA meetings. And the statements are modified each year by the staff and parents to reflect current thinking.

Note reference in the second statement of the school's mission to the "unique educational needs" of each child. The staff believes, foremost, that all children need to learn basic skills — that is, reading, writing, arithmetic. But, before this is possible, a third of the school's population must first learn English as a second language. Beyond that, the needs become more complicated and require elaboration. Garden Hills stated these needs as follows:

"The learning of American culture is an important need for all the students but especially to the new Americans by choice. The teaching of American history and geography, the democratic process, folklore and cultural arts are stressed. Because of this diverse population, all students also need human relations skills in order to develop an attitude of peaceful cooperation in resolving differences while learning to live together. Skills of communication (speaking, reading and writing) are therefore emphasized."

"Another need for all students is the development of behavior reflecting individual responsibility for and commitment to learning."

3.

Can, or will, a particular Garden Hills program achieve the goals the school has set up? Is the program meeting the needs of students?

Answers to these questions come from planning by individual staff members, by planning carried on in small groups and at faculty meetings or from a combination of all three.

An example of individual planning comes from my conversation with Rose Nichols, a first-grade teacher. I was able to talk with her one morning while her pupils were at physical education. She was so busy writing that I hesitated to interrupt her. When I asked her what she was doing, she said she was making out her plans for next week. She then told me that these plans served three purposes:

First, she herself would not do as good a job if she did not consciously lay out her plans a week at a time. Second, written plans not only keep Principal Geren up to date on what teachers expect to be doing in their classes next week, but they also give the principal an opportunity to suggest additional resources or to ask questions. In other words, written plans keep the principal close to the classrooms. The third reason for writing the plans is so that a substitute, who might be called upon unexpectedly because of the regular teacher's absence, will know where to begin, thereby saving both the substitute's and students' time.

Small group planning can occur at any opportunity. For example, the two fifth grade teachers often meet at breakfast to do their planning and the four kindergarten teachers meet regularly during lunch. Here is a case in point:

I asked Dr. Roby Egan, who was in his first year at Garden Hills, why the fourth kindergarten teacher had a different kind of assignment than the other three. He said that a problem arose in the fall when it became apparent that the increased enrollment of kindergartners would require the addition of another teacher. At first the three teachers who were already there were pleased to learn that the size of their classes would be reduced. But then they realized how much commotion would be caused by moving some children from each of the three kindergarten rooms on November 1 to create a fourth room headed by a new teacher. Shuffling the youngsters about so soon after school had started, while they were still in the process of becoming acquainted with their new surroundings and classmates, would have been unsettling.

Dr. Egan told me proudly of their solution, a decision made in a planning session by all four kindergarten teachers. The new teacher would work with all the kindergarteners in one subject — arithmetic. All of the children would then get acquainted with a second adult, and none of them would feel uneasy at being moved to another room.

Faculty meetings were held every Tuesday afternoon. This is the time when small group and individual planning are related to total staff planning. The agenda of the faculty meeting I attended is probably typical of these meetings. Dr. Geren began with an announcement of having secured a new portable classroom. This piece of news was greeted with applause, not only because the room was sorely needed but also because Dr. Geren had achieved this victory when portable classrooms were scarce.

Next followed an announcement by the computer manager, Barbara Johnson. She advised the teachers that she would soon be making an appointment with each of them to learn how well work in the computer room was meshing with work in the regular rooms.

Dr. Geren then made an announcement about a national campaign for child survival. This campaign, with former Presidents Gerald Ford and Jimmy Carter as honorary chairpersons, seemed important enough to deserve a short discussion. The school decided to assume a very active role in enabling pupils to learn about the conditions of poverty and starvation throughout the world. It also seemed apopropriate that the school should serve as the means by which the parents of Garden Hills pupils could become active in the campaign and share in its success. Later in the season Mrs. Rosalyn Carter visited the school and gave the campaign a more personal touch.

Next inservice opportunities for the second semester were discussed. "Inservice" and its equivalent "staff development" are important terms in Garden Hills and are the subject of frequent discussion among teachers. The terms refer to the fact that, like doctors, lawyers, administrators and business leaders, teachers must continually keep up to date on subject matter and how to teach. At the meeting I attended, Dr. Geren first told about a seminar at the University of Georgia at Athens which, although compulsory for principals, she thought might also be of interest to some teachers; and she identified seminar opportunities closer to home such as at Georgia State, Emory and other Atlanta universities and colleges.

The next subject to come to the floor for discussion revolved around the need to improve playground equipment and to beautify the campus with renovated gardens and shrubbery. Those who wanted to share in the scheduled work were invited to meet at the school the following Saturday.

After attending two faculty meetings, I was left with several impressions: first, at the beginning of each meeting, the teachers looked tired and worn out; next, during both meetings, Dr. Geren encouraged free discussion and the raising of questions and issues. I must add that in both instances the teachers looked less weary following the serving of refreshments.

At no time did Dr. Geren leave any doubt about where she stood: She was at the school's helm to make it a better one and that her major responsibility was to get on with the business of solving pressing problems which are always present. In my discussions with people at the school, I kept hearing one comment about Dr. Geren: "This principal never asks anyone to do anything that she isn't already doing herself or ready to start doing.

In addition to the planning input derived from a committed principal and staff, four activities help Garden Hills students maintain a high degree of academic performance:

The Atlanta school district administration reviews the progress of each school in attaining system-wide goals and provides it with a written report of its findings.

The school system also mandates an annual report of each pupil's progress which includes analysis of test results and degree of basic program and skills mastery.

Every spring a small team of the Garden Hills staff interviews the school's teachers to learn what subjects they think should be given high priority for the coming year; the team analyzes its findings and reports back to the faculty, and the faculty decides on priorities.

There is also an annual review of PTA and volunteer activities which concludes with recommendations for their continuation or changes for the next year.

Garden Hills has a staff development program which is practical as well as inspiring. One of them, called an ''artists-in-education'' program, was led by the talented husband and wife writing team, Richard Keeton and Sharyn Kane. Their primary aim was to help teachers improve the writing skills of students, teachers and parents, and to plant the seeds for appreciation of poetry and imaginative prose. During a recent year, from September 20 to December 20, these professionals served as writers-in-residence, conducting regular demonstration classes for students in creative writing while Garden Hills teachers observed, and conducting writing seminars for teachers as well as evening classes for adults interested in learning more about good writing.

This staff development activity was widely publicized. It was also well received. ''Mrs. Kane read a poem about a closet,'' Tami Wynkoop writes in a fall issue of the school newspaper. ''Mr. Keeton read a story about the 'Refrigerator Hall of Doom' which some kids in another school helped him to write. The program was good. I liked it when Richard Keeton was talking and Sharyn Kane was sticking her tongue out at him.''

Keeping staff development close to the needs of teachers is also illustrated by the computer program. Before the computer room began to operate, a two-day workshop was held for which Ms. Alberta Paul, recognized for her extensive experience in setting up computer programs, came from Washington, D. C. to provide training. One teacher representative from each grade and five special or support staff members attended the sessions.

This September workshop also provided staff members with an opportunity to become acquainted with Barbara Johnson, who would be the new computer lab manager. Ms. Johnson was selected because she knew a great deal about running a computer lab and was regarded as the kind of person who would be learning from the teachers while they were learning from her.

Teachers accompany their pupils to the lab. In turn, the lab manager meets individually with the teachers to learn what the youngsters are doing in their classrooms. The weekly newspaper featured the computer room in its October 4 issue, citing several student reactions:

> ''I didn't know how the keys went and how my fingers went to press the letters, but I went on and on and I got the hang of it.''

"We learned about touch typing, which means typing without looking at the keys. The best thing about the lab is that you get to work on your own computer."

"I played a math game with the computer and I won."

"I am looking forward to having a wonderful time learning keyboard skills."

But staff development opportunities are not confined to the school building or campus. The staff has found that travel pays educational dividends. Through travel, they are convinced, comes firsthand knowledge for their social studies teaching. A trip to Mexico one summer, for instance, made by Principal Geren and eight teachers, proved to be an especially rewarding experience because of the ideas teachers brought back with them for school use.

In the fall of 1985 two fourth grade teachers were given released time to "scout" Atlanta in preparation for a field trip planned for their pupils, an experience that helped them make decisions about the best bus route and places to eat along the way.

Each year the fifth grade takes a longer trip to round out its Garden Hills experiences — late in 1986 they would visit Washington D. C. In August of the same year, the teachers who would be sponsoring this trip were also among the group representing their school at the U. S. Department of Education recognition ceremonies in the capital. Before coming home, however, they toured Washington so they could decide more specifically what to visit and what to observe when they brought their pupils to the capital later in the year.

Recognizing the importance of staff development, the Atlanta school system provides funds to individual schools for development of programs or projects which relate to system-wide goals. One of these goals is helping students learn how to think and reason. It's one thing to have "learned" something by rote and another to have learned "how" to think and reason. For example, in 1984 Dr. William Geren, university professor and husband of Garden Hills Principal Peggy Geren, conducted a workshop for the Garden Hills staff in which the Socratic method was discussed as a way to support higher order thinking. This method, which emphasizes the importance of questioning instead of telling, has wide support as a sound approach to teaching and learning.

Staff development at Garden Hills can be described as being tailormade inasmuch as each staff member is primarily responsible for deciding best ways to keep up with new subject matter and better ways to conduct lessons. But the principal is always at hand to suggest new avenues for personal and professional growth. She encourages staff members to participate in activities beyond the school which expand teacher horizons and enhance professional skills. For example, Sally Lovein, who heads up English as a Second Language (ESL) at Garden Hills, has written an article on multicultural education for *Georgia's Children*, a publication of the Georgia Association on Young Children.

Recruitment of first-rate teachers is essential in building a staff capable of delivering quality leadership. But good schools, to stay good, need even more. They need people who will continue to grow in service, who will engage in a life time of learning.

Inasmuch as the school district gives Dr. Geren major hiring responsibilities for Garden Hills, she had opportunities in 1984 and 1985 to recruit seven classroom teachers. It is evident from her selections that she tries to provide a balance and depth in staff to more completely meet the needs of the pupils.

Two of the seven teachers who were employed during that period were inexperienced. One was selected from the master graduates at an Atlanta university because of her outstanding scholastic record and personal qualities. The second, a native of Puerto Rico, was employed as she completed her master's at Emory University.

Adding up the total years of professional experience of the other five recruits, we arrive at 62 years — with 12 years being the average. Two of them have their Ph.D.s; three their master's; while two are still working on their master's.

They came from teacher education institutions as far west as UCLA and as far north as Wayne University in Detroit. Their main emphasis in graduate work has been early childhood education, but having jobs in the world of work and homemaking as background also seemed to appeal to Dr. Geren. Several of them list volunteer community service jobs in their resumes.

After becoming acquainted with these teachers, I would generalize that the qualities they all possess are a commitment to education as a profession, and personal traits which include caring, willingness to work hard and a realistic kind of intelligence.

But there is more to developing an excellent school than having an excellent staff, and the principal and teachers at Garden Hills recognize the role that parents and community leaders play. Next we'll examine how the school teamed up with the home and the community.

4.

Not content to be a little school lost in a big city, Garden Hills appears eager to learn as much as it can about Atlanta and to capitalize on the resources of this metropolitan area. In the process, Garden Hills has become a working partner with the parents of the school and with leaders throughout the community.

Installation of a computer center in 1985-86 exemplifies what good things can happen to a school with community help. A former Garden Hills student, and now a prominent Atlanta businessman, Mr. Scott Seidel spearheaded an effort resulting in the gift of a $250,000 center for computer-based instruction (Plato-Wicat). Installed in a refurbished classroom, the equipment consists of a main frame computer, thirty keyboards and monitors with audio capability.

Two businesses (Coopers and Lybrand, an international accounting firms; and the English Language Center at Lenox Square) provide volunteer services for career exploration and social studies enrichment as well as funds for materials and supplies for social studies classes.

To a remarkable degree, the PTA at Garden Hills is a "working" unit. Eighteen members head up committees that work on school programs and problems. On six of these committees, the PTA members team up with a teacher to lead a particular program, such as the artists-in-residence sessions previously described.

Several Garden Hills parents, in addition to providing effective PTA leadership, are active in community-wide organizations known as NAPPS (North Atlanta Parents for Public Schools) and the APPLE (Atlanta Parents and Public Linked for Education) Corps, which are discussed later.

The staff and PTA executive committee leaders work together in securing volunteers for various phases of specific school programs. When I visited one of the regular classrooms I generally saw a parent, or several, working one-on-one with a pupil needing special help. Parent volunteers also serve the school in many other ways. They assist in the media center and ESL (English as a Second Language) summer school, chaperone field trips, and help to landscape and keep the school grounds beautiful. Volunteers are recruited primarily from the families of students but additional help also comes from a neighboring senior high school and the community at large.

The participation of parents is not limited to helping pupils. They also advise the staff in many ways. At least two conferences are held each year with the parent and the pupil's teacher, and comments from these conferences — as well as feedback on report cards — play an important role in future planning sessions regarding curriculum changes and budgetary considerations.

Parents also participate in selecting textbooks and other instructional materials as when they help select books for RIF (Reading Is Fundamental), a program sponsored by the U. S. Department of Education, underwritten by Lever Brothers and designed to make young people aware of the fun of reading.

The PTA is often involved in efforts to raise money for enrichment programs if and when the Atlanta school district budget runs out. When the general fund budget for school supplies and book allocations is depleted, for instance, the PTA may come to the rescue. Or when Garden Hills must release teachers for a specific staff development activity, PTA financial help may make that possible.

I remember an assembly I attended starring Kermit Love of Sesame Street Actors in a program called "Adventures of Snuggle." "Snuggle," a bear puppet, and Love's performance brought down the house with applause. The highlight of the program came when each pupil was given a small bear to take home and snuggle.

One had to wonder where the money for the program — and the bears — came from, and to whom to give thanks. The pleasure derived by each child from this small gift and the program itself undoubtedly spurred reading interest. Later I learned that the school's contribution was underwritten by the PTA. Lever Bros. and other sources beyond Atlanta underwrote the remaining cost.

In numerous ways, Garden Hills' PTA takes an active role in its school's activities. When I attended one of the PTA meetings in 1986, the treasurer reported that candy sales and other money-raising projects had increased the treasury balance to $7,700. Then, the PTA president reminded the group of projects for which commitments had been made. Money had already been allocated for new and rebuilt playground equipment. Needs for a Xerox machine and new curtains for the auditorium stage were identified. Action was taken to purchase the curtains and to rent the Xerox machine. The next two subjects dealt with PTA participation: how to increase male involvement and attendance by parents who live long distances from the school.

Dr. Geren then explained the Iowa Test of Basic Skills which was soon to be given to the pupils. She also told the parents about an invitation that had been extended to Garden Hills pupils to ride on the Georgia Education Association float, pointing out that this was an honor since only three schools in the state had been invited to participate in the float. The parents quickly reacted by agreeing to provide the necessary transportation and supervision for involved pupils.

Garden Hills PTA, I think, is unique in its organization of working committees. At least five of these committees consist of a parent and a teacher who work as a team to direct a particular program.

The artists-in-residence program, for instance, is headed up by PTA member Terry Millkey and Sally Lovein, the teacher responsible for English as a Second Language. This program is sponsored by the National Endowment for the Arts, the Georgia Council for the Arts, and by the PTA. In bargaining with the Georgia Council, when the PTA emphasized that its budget had already been allocated, PTA's original projected commitment for the artists' program was reduced from $3,200 to $2,100, with the money to be raised outside the regular PTA budget.

Although two business firms and several staff members and parents had already contributed, the PTA was still far from its goal of $2,100. But — hold on — there was good news. At one meeting Milkey reported an anonymous pledge of $500 if an equal amount was forthcoming from private contributors. And good news it was, for those contributions, together with the funds raised by a wine-tasting event in which the parents had an opportunity to meet the artists-in-residence, Mr. and Mrs. Keeton, produced the needed $2,100.

Other committees, or programs, headed by a team consisting of a parent and a teacher include the cultural arts committee which provides funds for children to go to off-campus events such as the performances by the Children's Theater and the Atlantic Symphony, and those programs provided by Young Audiences. In addition to these double-chaired committees, Garden Hills PTA boasts other working committees, as I discovered at 8:00 one morning when I stopped at the school store to buy some supplies and was surprised to find a PTA parent already on duty — "minding" the store. Other committees headed by parents deal with chocolate sales, health and safety, hospitality, recruitment, publicity, photography, new parent liaison, library and the international dinner which requires three parents to chair because of the magnitude of the project.

Committee heads work with PTA officers who include two co-presidents (to ensure that at least one is available when a decision has to be made and carried out quickly), two vice-presidents, a treasurer, two secretaries, international representatives (a couple whose child is learning English as a second language) and a faculty representative for the executive committee.

At one of the PTA meetings I attended, officers permitted me to ask parents for their reactions to the question, "Why do you think Garden Hills is a good school?" The multicultured mix of the student body was mentioned by 20 parents; 15 commented on the ability and managing skills of the principal and added that the professional and well-educated faculty made the school outstanding; 12 included the caring and positive atmosphere of the school. During my stay at the school, I was privileged to observe first-hand how these forces work together to provide that atmosphere.

5.

I was at Garden Hills at the time the fourth grade classes visited Atlanta. Their excitement about what they had seen and heard on this field trip was recounted over and over in what students wrote and spoke long after the trip was a memory. They had discovered things about Atlanta that they wanted to communicate, and I noticed that this same enthusiasm was evident in the kindergartners after their trip to the planetarium.

One project in a fifth grade room involves taking the students to a movie on a Friday night. Aside from the fact that the movie is selected for its high quality and important message, the teacher considers this an important outing for still another reason. Because her students live in several parts of Atlanta and do not have a chance to play together after school or on weekends, she feels that this social event gives them a chance to become more friendly and understanding of each other. As the teacher phrased it, "It develops their sense of community."

The community not only enters the school to enhance learning but it also brings pupils into the community for the same reason. The celebration of Martin Luther King Week illustrates an example of how this two-way flow strengthens the partnership between Garden Hills and its homes and community. Spurred on by national TV exposure as well as information gained from local sources, students are often taken by their parents to visit the memorial that has been established in King's honor in Atlanta, his hometown.

Another example is the International Children's Folk Dance Group (meeting after school one afternoon each week) which performs before many civic groups, including nursing and retirement homes, and even appeared one Christmas Eve on the renowned national TV program, "Nightline."

The Garden Hills staff recognizes that the most effective way to develop responsibility in students and commitment to others is through participation in real-life experiences. This is one of the reasons teachers encourage fifth grade pupils to help kindergartners learn to read. Older pupils participated in the "Heart Trek Race," a UNICEF project which raised $400 to help relieve world hunger. Garden Hills students also wanted to take an active role in celebrating the Statue of Liberty's hundredth birthday, so they went to work and donated their hard-earned $200 to the gala event. Still another time, when a school employee lost everything in a Christmas night fire, the entire school's energies and resources poured out to help the family in its tragic hours of need.

So many things go on at Garden Hills that tie the school to home and the community that it is difficult to list them all. It's a little like the movies' Academy Award Winners who, in their acceptance speeches, try to name everyone who made the slightest contribution to their success. Some of the school's most popular community events are the receptions held at the home of Principal Geren and at the school. In addition, annual celebrations staged during an entire week, when pupils dramatize the cultures of their native countries and share their writing, art and costumes, are enjoyed by members of the community. Highlight of this event is its international dinner.

Then there is "Play Day," that one day in May of each year during which the community, as well as the school, is treated to an action-packed demonstration of the skills learned in physical education.

Rather than bemoaning the bureaucracy of the Atlanta school district or of the state government — both of which necessarily must provide guidelines and regulations for individual schools — the staff and parents of Garden Hills strive to work with the state and district officials for the benefit of the school.

6.

Atlanta's Area III leadership not only cooperates with Garden Hills in the school's efforts to achieve system-wide objectives but also supports the school en route to broader goals that go beyond the school district statement. A lot of credit for the success of this cooperative alliance must go to the Georgia State Department of Education and its staff of educators.

Beyond this alliance lies the fact that Georgians in general take seriously their responsibility to elect political leaders who understand the importance of good schools. There is no other logical explanation for some of the good things that happen at Garden Hills. Take the subject of reading. Every thinking person agrees that to read is of first importance in any school. The Georgia State Department of Education thinks it is so important that it warrants special attention and has adopted a Basic Curriculum Content reading program which is coordinated with statewide testing. Central to the program is the state's document, "Basic Curriculum Content," with supplementary textbooks and materials added as necessary to achieve goals of the reading program.

The Houghton Mifflin Reading Series, consisting of booklets graduated from Level A through M and then 13 and 14, was being used in 1985. It must have been working well as indicated by the high reading test scores of Garden Hills pupils.

As I observed and talked with students during these reading sessions, I was surprised to discover that the big thing on their minds was the book that they were reading and when they might be ready to tackle the next book in the series.

To better understand this eagerness, it is helpful to back up a little. The Atlanta public schools have developed a Pupil Progression Plan that asks the question, "If a student is not promoted, will he or she have to repeat material already mastered?" The answer is no — because Atlanta subscribes to the proposition that students will continue their work at their own level of mastery sometimes referred to as the "diagnostic-prescriptive continuing learning process." Garden Hills, therefore, encourages readers to move through the series of books at a pace deemed best for the individual student by the teacher.

One little boy in the second grade had to tell me about the book he was reading titled, *Sunburst*. From this encounter, I was surprised and pleased to learn that when a first grader is ready for *Sunburst*, which is a second grade level book, he or she is encouraged to tackle it regardless of the technicality of grade status. And this same wisdom applies at the other end of the spectrum. If a second grader has not grasped reading level F by the time he or she moves into the third grade, *Sunburst* would be on the docket in the third grade.

Although this kind of learning approach seems on the surface to have the blessings of the state, the school district and Garden Hills in general, some kindergarten teachers believe that regularized and formalized pre-reading is started too soon. The Atlanta district requires that a written form be completed by the teacher to document kindergarten pre-reading performance objectives for each child. This form contains 22 categories — ready steps, visual discrimination steps, auditory discrimination, language experience, writing — to name a few. Under these headings are included such topics as sequencing, upper case letter forms, letter-vowel sounds, verbs and nouns, and writing your first name.

Kindergarten teachers told me that one of their toughest jobs is to help parents understand that children can be pressured to master reading at too early an age. Some are not quite ready to cope with reading for a variety of reasons — their home experiences may have been scant or their interest in the printed word is at a low level. Each year, as each new crop of youngsters begins school, these issues of how to teach them to read come up again and again.

But the teachers convey confidence and optimism that through the efforts of their principal, Dr. Geren, the current reading policy will be examined as required at regional and district-wide levels of the Atlanta school system.

7.

Just because a school is small in size does not mean it can not aspire to big deeds. Garden Hills, with the help of two organizations, NAPPS and the APPLE Corps, demonstrates how this one small school can exert extensive influence through an enlarging set of concentric circles.

For example, between 1970 and 1980, as the city schools were integrated, white enrollment in the Atlanta school district plummeted by 33,000 students. But a group of northside parents decided they would not allow their children to become part of the white-flight statistics, and to show their determination to support one another, they formed NAPPS which stands for North Atlanta Parents for Public Schools.

High on the list of NAPPS priorities is its commitment to do everything possible and practical to maintain good balance between white and black enrollment regardless of location of the schools. NAPPS seeks to attract students from private schools, but the myth that public schools cannot equal private schools academically is hard to eradicate.

Dr. Geren and her staff keep in close touch with NAPPS and support its work. "Support Public Schools" car bumper stickers tell other drivers where NAPPS members stand on school issues and problems. Production and distribution of its color brochure for northside residents carries the importance of the message even closer to home. But NAPPS doesn't stop there.

The Atlanta school district's Garden Hills, five other elementary schools, two middle schools and two high schools, hold open houses for residents to get better acquainted with NAPPS programs and objectives. As many as 500 people have attended such open houses. Beyond those, the city-wide performing arts gala held annually at Lenox Square leaves little doubt in the minds of public school parents that the young people in their district are doing a remarkable job with their acting, dancing and singing abilities.

Parents, of course, being parents, are always weighing the pros and cons of the best place to send their children to school. This dilemma was brought home in a March 1983 article published in *In Town Extra*, a weekly insert in the *Atlanta Constitution* and *Journal*. In it a parent describes the favorable differences she observed in her daughter's school outlook and performance after removing her from a private school and placing her back in a public school.

APPLE (Atlanta Parents and Public Linked for Education) Corps, a district-wide organization for parents and interested citizens, sponsors workshops, gives mini-grants to schools and monitors school board meetings.

Garden Hills is fortunate in being able to participate in activities that do not confine it to district and/or state levels but are also national in scope. For instance, Jean Young, the mayor's wife who chairs the mayor's task force on education, is also the national chairperson of UNICEF. In this capacity, she visits Garden Hills several times a year, and each time she says that when she sees here the U.N. type of student body — learning and living — her inspiration and motivation are renewed.

While Mrs. Young seeks the counsel of Principal Peggy Geren as she pursues her various civic responsibilities in connection with the mayor's task force on education, Dr. Geren in turn taps the resources available to the mayor's wife, and between the two of them good things happen. One of these good things revolves around the Corporation for Entertainment and Learning, Inc. (CEL) of New York City which is developing a 20th century video library. With the help of Mrs. Young, Garden Hills was able to enter into a cooperative arrangement with CEL to test out certain library resources. This project, now located in the Garden Hills media center, is being monitored by a fifth grade teacher.

I was amazed at the ease with which this collection makes it possible for Garden Hills teachers to identify, secure and project a videotape in their classrooms, bringing to life invaluable pictorial documentation of important segments of history, such as President John Kennedy's innaugural address. There appears to be no limit to its application. How can we put a price on the value of this acquisition as an example of how one small school can profit from a national resource?

The ways in which contributions between Garden Hills and the outside world flow in two directions are many and diverse. At first it wouldn't seem that Atlanta schools in general and Garden Hills in particular and the Western Interstate Commission for Higher Education and the National Council for Educational Research would have anything in common, but they do — they all want to keep in touch firsthand with what is happening in American education that might enhance teaching and learning.

33

Dr. Harold L. Enarson, president emeritus of Ohio State University, upon concluding his visits of Atlanta schools and Garden Hills as a representative of the last two organizations previously named, recognized this common denominator. He had high praise for the school system's unique features: its goal approach to teaching, its high degree of parental involvement, and its success in bringing 120 businesses into the Atlanta partnership of business and education — most of which Dr. Enarson attributed to the efforts of school superintendent, Dr. Alonzo Crim. To date, 51 businesses have "adopted" schools.

In his tour of Garden Hills, Enarson was guided by a pupil who proudly told the guest that there were 22 countries represented in the first grade class at Garden Hills. But that was before Dr. Enarson discovered a shy, brown-haired boy from Russia who was just starting his first week, whereupon he tactfully corrected his small guide with, "We now have 23."

Enarson summed up his visit. "All were learning English. It is a thrilling sight. The building is old, comfortable and clean. The vibrations are all good."

Garden Hills reaps its greatest wealth of favorable publicity from columnists and reporters of the city's major daily newspaper, the *Atlanta Constitution*. One of these columnists is Celestine Sibley who also happens to have two grandchildren attending Garden Hills. These are some of the thoughts she shared with her Atlanta readers about the holiday activities in late December of 1985:

> "Children's voices fill the air with Christmas spirit . . . The other morning I took a roast out of the oven long before it was ready and struck out for town, roast bleeding, and darkness all around me, to be sure to get to the Garden Hills Elementary School's Christmas program."
> "It was worth it," as Dr. Peggy Geren, the principal, pointed out."
> "You're not really ready for Christmas until you've heard little children sing." She was counting on her young pupils filling her with the Christmas spirit, and I was, too. And it happened.
> "David and John Steven (columnist Sibley's grand-children) have been singing Christmas songs for weeks, not really carols in the sense of hymns to the birth of the baby Jesus, for this is a well-mixed school with children of all races and faiths participating in the program. So we had no 'Away in a Manger' and no 'Silent Night'. Instead, there were German, English, Mexican, Spanish, French, Hebrew and Hasidic folk songs. And it was perfectly lovely."

Later, Dr. Geren told me, "We make a special effort to respect each student's beliefs during the holiday season. The music is not only from the Christian tradition but also from the Jewish and other cultures."

Atlanta Constitution staff writer Beverly Barnes gave considerable space to the trip that Garden Hills teachers and principal would soon be taking to Mexico. The Barnes' feature story, "Ole! Atlanta Teachers to Visit Mexico," described how the staff felt about the trip. "We want to improve not only our instruction," one staff member was quoted, "but also the way we relate to the children in our multi-cultural environment. We think it will have an impact on all of us, even those who are not going. We are confident that what we bring back will carry over to all the students.'' The article also stated that the cost of the trip ($700, excluding meals) would be borne by each of the staff members making the trip.

But there is another newspaper upon which the school relies to insure that all affected people keep up with what is ''going on'' at Garden Hills. This newspaper is called *Bullpup Bulletin* and is published weekly at the school by parents, teachers, and pupils.

Each issue of the *Bullpup* (named by pupils in a school-wide contest) contains a short article by the principal. During the year 1985-1986 some of the subjects covered by Dr. Geren were the importance of study habits, safety in the buses, the student government working with various rooms in developing rules for an orderly learning environment, Book Week and the significance of social studies. Another time she wrote of Thanksgiving as a special time to remember others, and a piece in a January issue explored the opportunities that a new year gives for looking at ourselves and deciding on changes that we need to make.

Bullpup is read by pupils, parents, and teachers. Although Principal Geren's weekly messages are generally beamed at pupils, they may also contain ideas on how parents can help the school and their children. On the other hand, some articles in the weekly newsletter are directed especially to parents, such as the announcement that soon Garden Hills would be offering free English classes for parents whose first language is not English.

In these pages I have tried to describe the various and unique kinds of partnerships that exist at Garden Hills. Through such partnerships Garden Hills seems to have become a school where three groups — parents, community citizens and staff — have discovered that each can do its particular job best by working in concert with the other two to introduce youngsters to the joys of learning.

Like the familiar maxim about overlooking the obvious (''can't see the forest for the trees''), cooperation between home, community and school appears to be so much a part of the warp and woof of everyday activities at Garden Hills that no one involved individual seems to give it a second thought.

8.

You will recall that Garden Hills develops a statement of the primary needs of pupils and also reduces to writing the mission of the school as the staff and parents see it.

The staff's statements of needs and goals include the acquisition of certain skills (communication, computation, problem-solving and citizenship), knowledge, attitudes, and appreciations. Nothing too unusual about that, you say — isn't that what most schools are supposed to be striving for? Yes, but Garden Hills goes a step further. It strives to imbue its students with a commitment to learning, emphasizing their responsibility for self-directed learning.

Practicing the skills needed as a global citizen is particularly important for Garden Hills with its pupils of many nationalities. In the pages that follow we shall discover how the school as a whole and its individual classes meet the needs of these pupils in order to prepare them for living in the 21st century.

Garden Hills staff members feel certain that they can provide good teaching only as they get to know their students. To accomplish this, teachers try to work with children on a one-to-one basis; but when the whole group is in the room, sometimes a pat on the back or a smile of appreciation for something well done has to suffice. And sometimes, while pupils are studying or reading on their own, the teacher is conferring with a single pupil. Some of the teachers capitalize on time available to do this when pupils are at breakfast or waiting in the gymnasium for school to begin. Or a teacher will arrange, a day ahead of time, for a conference in the regular classroom during a certain period. Or time may be utilized while the class moves on to meet with a different teacher in another room, and the classroom teacher makes arrangements for a child to stay behind to confer in private.

Parent conferences offer excellent opportunities for teachers to learn even more about each of their students, and conferences are serious business at Garden Hills. A form is sent home to the parent, asking for a convenient conference time and what specific questions the parents would like to discuss. I asked one teacher how she felt about these meetings — did they really help in getting to know all of her parents? "Yes," she said, "except when they are unable to come to the school, but we do a pretty good job of getting acquainted by telephone."

Pupils with whom I spoke told me they feel respected at Garden Hills — they don't feel like so many numbers, forced to be there only to learn certain facts and skills. When I asked the fifth grade students to write out what they regarded Garden Hills' most outstanding characteristic, twelve of them wrote "the teachers." Three listed friendliness, and another three mentioned internationalism. The other responses were scattered among topics such as availability of computers, physical education and field trips.

I also asked if they had any suggestions for improvements in the school. Seventeen answered that the school site and playground should be kept in better shape, and five mentioned the need to improve the cafeteria and its menus. The only other topics mentioned more than once were "We should have more physical education," "We should have more computer time," "We should have more books and more time in the library."

I found it amazing that none of the respondents made negative statements about their principal, their teachers or the way they were treated by any of them. Surely, I had thought, there must be something the matter with someone in this place! But the more I thought about it, the more I understood. I found the answer in an incident one of the teachers told me had happened while she was a guest at the home of Dr. Geren, along with other teachers and parents who had been invited for an informal "get-together."

Also present that evening was first-grader Omeed, the son of an American mother and an Iranian father, and there presumably because his parents were unable to find a sitter for him.

At the end of the evening the principal asked if anyone had anything they wanted to say before they went home. Several parents and two or three of the teachers made brief comments. Then, Omeed slowly raised his hand.

His shyness made it difficult for him to begin. "Little boys and girls come to school so frightened — they don't know what to expect. I came and had the most wonderful time. Everybody has been so loving and I have learned so much. I just wanted to say 'thank you' to everybody."

Omeed was obviously an unusual first grader to have bravely seized that moment to express the way he felt about his school. But he answered the question I had in my mind about the lack of negativism on the part of the students when I asked them what they liked or disliked about their school. Omeed's sentiments reflected what many Garden Hills pupils feel — loved.

9.

The Garden Hills staff must agree with the researcher at Columbia University who once stated that every child can do something better than 50 percent of the other children. What he meant, of course, was that if a school has a varied and rich enough program, every child can succeed at *something*.

Opportunities flourish for students to be recognized for achievement at Garden Hills. These are some of the accolades and laurels bestowed on pupils during 1984-1985:

    City-wide science and social science recognition awards
    Books written by students judged superior and excellent by district
       teams
    Choral and string musicians judged superior in city-wide competition
    Art pieces selected for display in four different art exhibits
    Twenty students chosen to participate in the opening of the exhibit,
       "China, 7000 Years of Discovery," during Georgia Institute of
       Technology's 100th anniversary celebration
    Garden Hills chorus performance in an ABC-TV national program on
       Christmas Eve
    Selection by three organizations for the international dancers and
       chorus to perform

In addition to recognitions given in the individual rooms for good citizenship and good behavior, a poster outside the auditorium announces the star citizen of the month, an activity sponsored by the student council and coordinated by the staff. Three rules lay the groundwork for judging: Arrive on time, pay attention and be committed to learning. And there are also special movies for rooms whose students excel in behavior.

On the other side of the coin, how Garden Hills deals with matters when everything is not "just great" also deserves attention. We could start with the cafeteria which, because it is small and used often, presents a variety of problems. To deal with them, members of the student council sponsor discussions and make recommendations for improvement. Then council observers monitor how well their suggestions have succeeded in improving conditions.

Conduct on school buses is not always A-1 either. In the space of two years, Garden Hills had two suspensions for poor conduct on buses. But not long after the student council took on a project aimed at improving bus conduct, fewer warnings were issued. The following year there were no suspensions because of misbehavior on the bus. This dramatic improvement was the result of council energies (with teacher leadership) concentrating on displays of bus rules, attention-getting posters, and an original playlet that was presented at a school-wide assembly.

In "basic" rooms, disciplinary control is worked out by each teacher with the cooperation of pupils. Visiting one class, I noticed at the front of the room, on the left side, a poster bearing a very sad face; on the right side, a second poster with a happy face. I asked a pupil what they meant. He said that the names under the sad face were those of pupils who had done something wrong. Those named under the happy face were students who had done something outstanding to make for happy living in the room.

I asked him what happens to those named on either of the two lists; and what about the people whose names don't appear on either list? He explained that the teacher organizes a small party for those on the happy list and generally invites all of the others who are not on either list to join the party.

As for the "bad" guys — well, he told me the penalty for those whose names appeared on the sad list is to sit on the wall outside the building and watch others play. To this young informant, sitting on the wall while watching others play, appeared to be harsh punishment.

While we discussed discipline one teacher told me that she tries to help pupils realize the relationship between enjoyable activities and those which are more clearly work, and that you can't have one without the other. "For example," she said, "we know that all parts of the reading program are not equally interesting. One of my students heard from some of the others that a particular book was especially interesting, but it was my decision that he would have to work hard at mastering some additional skills that I thought he needed before I would let him read that book."

Basic rooms at Garden Hills, where pupils spend most of their time, are homelike and attractive. Teachers encourage students to help make the room into a school home. Housekeeping chores, greeting visitors and making them comfortable, and assisting the teacher by entering scores on various charts hanging on the walls are the kinds of jobs students eagerly volunteer to undertake.

Drawings and paintings, together with a colorful display of other items to highlight each season of the year, add to the appeal of each room. School-wide poster displays often emphasize a particular person or event, thereby stimulating resources for study. This was done, for example, during one January when Martin Luther King's birthday commemoration provided the theme for displays in every room.

How Garden Hills is governed is a major concern of the student council. The group meets weekly with its faculty sponsor. Here is a glimpse of a typical student council meeting:

Old business dealt with making valentine cards for senior citizens in retirement homes. One student volunteered to make some calls and to report back at the next meeting. New business: Any ideas for "special" days? Answer: Members liked the idea of a Cowgirl and Cowboy Day. Next move: Council members would talk with their homerooms to get reactions to a Cowgirl and Cowboy Day, as well as solicit suggestions for other ideas for a special day.

The concerns of the student council cover a wide range — from helping the school employee mentioned earlier whose home burned down Christmas night — to working with Mrs. Rosalyn Carter when she came to the school to appeal for help from students and parents on a project aimed at alleviating hunger and poor health among Third World children.

Other student organizations carry on a variety of activities. One of the most popular is the school newspaper. But the Garden Hills newspaper does more than keep students, parents and staff up to date, which is its main objective. Students also derive experience as they participate in its publication.

A look at several issues of *Bullpup Bulletin* tells us a lot about the kind of young people at work here. This particular issue highlights the excellence recognition won by the school and the trip taken to the nation's capital by representatives of the school staff and parents.

In addition to articles for staff and parents, it contains two drawings: one of a magnificent eagle and the words, "Excellence in Education 1985-1986," contributed by student Vu Hoan; and the other by Meranee Phingvodhipakkiya and Jessica Nations. This drawing throws a spotlight on Mr. James Jones, retiring custodian, and beneath the art work begins an article about Mr. Jones by the same two students.

Then there is a full column devoted to two games created by students Rahman Howard and Wayne Wu, — a word puzzle and a word search — which were based on facts about Washington D. C.

A regular feature, always of interest to the pupils, called "What's Cookin'?" contains the cafeteria menu for the following week. The social calendar announces that the first meeting of the international dance group will be next Monday.

The issue ends with an invitation for suggestions and comments, and a reminder that the deadline for submitting material is 4:30 Wednesday afternoon. *Bullpup Bulletin* is then ready for distribution on Friday — just two working days later.

It's an air of enthusiasm you can't possibly miss at Garden Hills — this awareness that the pupils feel that it is *their* school — *their* community. The staff and parents work overtime to maintain this enthusiasm. This is accomplished with activities such as the cultural arts program which enriches classroom experiences while at the same time provides genuine enjoyment. Managed by a teacher-parent team, this program, for parents who can afford it, costs $5 per year; the PTA picks up the tab for the balance.

As part of the cultural arts program, several Young Audiences programs are presented at the school. Young Audiences is a nationally based non-profit organization whose goals are two-fold: to instill an appreciation of the arts "which will last a lifetime" and to help discover the potential of individual children as performers. (Address: 115 E. 92 Street, New York, New York 10128)

Its record is impressive. In 1984 Young Audiences reached nearly 4 million school children, training about 2,000 professional performers to go into the schools to work with students and their teachers. Encouraged by Young Audiences' commitment to unlock young people's creativity and inventive abilities, corporations and foundations also contribute to its budget.

While I visited Garden Hills, one of the Young Audiences' programs featured Sioux Indian culture with Chief Red Dawn and his adopted son, Blue Eagle. From my vantage point, the audience appeared spellbound as the Chief, an anthropologist, told stories that introduced elements of the Indian sign language. Later, Indian dancing gave the students an insight into Sioux culture. As I left the auditorium, a Young Audiences representative handed me a booklet, its front page carrying this message: "Young Audiences puts dance, music, and theater where they belong — in the heads, hearts, and hands of children."

Representative students are asked to help in evaluating what programs might be approved for presentation by Young Audiences. So it was that in the fall of 1985 fourth and fifth grade students were invited to preview a variety of shows, including dance, theater and musicals for possible presentation at the school. Their reactions to this preview were used in selecting future programs. Here are some of their comments about what they had seen:

> "The Puppeteers put on a show about how to make a healthy body, which I enjoyed a lot. The puppets showed good food with protein, iron, minerals and calories."

"I think the best dancers were the Ruth Mitchell Dancers . . . It was neat to see Cooter from 'Dukes of Hazard', who served as host."

The cultural program also includes a variety of off-campus treats. Dennis LoRusso writes in the *Bullpup Bulletin* about one of the concerts he attended:

"On January 8 the third, fourth and fifth graders went to hear the Atlanta Symphony Orchestra. The symphony played music by the musical genius Wolfgang Amadeus Mozart. Another piece featured a symphony about animals called 'The Carnival of Animals.' Probably the favorite was John Phillip Sousa's march, 'The Washington Post.' It was a very exciting trip."

Some cultural programs, on the other hand, may originate at Garden Hills, such as the entertainment provided by the school's international dancing group. Consisting of third and fourth graders, these rhythmic artists meet once a week after school with Mrs. Ethel Rutledge, their teacher-leader for the past eight years. The PTA underwrites a nominal stipend for Mrs. Rutledge.

Appreciation for this activity is evident from the number of former students who sometimes drop by to watch dance rehearsals. Mrs. Rutledge's dancers have entertained a variety of groups — something of which they are very proud. In addition, she also finds much satisfaction in knowing that one of her alumni has received a scholarship to the Harlem Dance Theater.

I visited a second grade room one day in mid-January and talked with a student who had volunteered to help me learn what his class did throughout the day. Our conversation almost at an end, he leaned over and whispered in my ear that, although his classmates were not supposed to know, he had been invited to read his poem about Martin Luther King over the loud-speaker system on Dr. King's birthday — and he urged me to listen. It came through clear and strong:

> Dr. Martin Luther King
> Married a woman who used to sing;
> Her name was Coretta Scott;
> They loved each other a lot.
>
> When he got his school degree,
> Martin Luther King fought to be FREE!
> He fought until he was thirty-three;
> He fought for equality.
>
> Then he fought for six more years;
> Then everybody wept with tears
> When he got shot in the head;
> Martin Luther King was dead.
>
> All over the world people cried;
> Martin Luther King had died.

Later that day I went into my young guide's second grade room. I expressed my appreciation to him for having written a fine poem and complimented him on delivering it in such a clear and courageous voice. He asked me if I would like a copy of it, and I said, "Certainly." He said, "I can't type well enough, but my friend here has typed it for me, and I would like to give you this xeroxed copy." From then on — let's call him Ben — Ben and I recognized each other whenever we passed in the halls, or I was led to believe we did by waving at one another. I became confused when I visited a different second grade room several days later because I was certain I saw Ben there too, busily studying, but he didn't wave when he saw me. Must have been transferred, I thought. On inquiry, however, I found that Ben and his identical twin brother were both attending Garden Hills!

Several questions surface when we begin to analyze why Garden Hills students scored high on the California Achievement Test in grades one through five. In 1983 the median was at the 83rd percentile. By 1984 this reached the 91st percentile; and in 1985 the 94th percentile. With the 50th percentile being par, these scores are impressive.

Why are achievement scores so high?

Why are so many students transferring back to Garden Hills from private schools?

How can students give the impression of being happy and serious-minded at the same time?

Why did three metropolitan newspaper articles report that the school's "vibrations" were good?

I decided there was no better way to get answers to these questions than to ask the teachers themselves, so I started with, "What do you think is outstanding about Garden Hills?" Answers given more than twice included:

Unique student population

Warmth and concern for others

Supportive, involved and professional administration

Supportive PTA

Extra "givingness" of the staff

Another question I asked the staff was, "What would you like to see changed at Garden Hills?" Twenty-two of the answers referred to the school site or equipment; only two other answers appeared as often as twice: Reduce pupil-teacher ratio and improve cafeteria behavior.

With the classroom obviously the central place where learning occurs, an analysis of the reasons for Garden Hills being a good school reveals these observations:

Classrooms are busy, yet friendly, work places.

The work is challenging.

3R's are learned in a setting of meaningful experiences.

Teachers feel on their own and are responsible for the quality of learning in their classrooms.

42

10.

Upon entering a classroom, pupils understand that they have four work choices while the teacher is busy with routine beginning-of-the-period jobs: They can either

write in their journal which each pupil keeps or

choose a book to read or

read the schedule of work for the day which is already on the blackboard or

choose something else to study from their desks, such as spelling.

Teachers at Garden Hills acknowledge the emotional as well as the intellectual needs of pupils. An atmosphere prevails in which the pupils sense that teachers care for them, that they believe in them and like them. Under stress, therefore, pupils will come to the teacher just as they would go to their parents at home.

Children need to exercise their large muscles, which translates into "A long period without a change makes for restlessness and discipline problems." Within the room children can, on an individual and informal basis, go to any part of the room when they have reason to do so. The basic teacher often works with a small group — generally a third of the class — while the other two-thirds are working at their seats. Adding these shifts in motion within the room to the movement created by students going to and from classes taught by other teachers, and to lunch and play periods, ensures that the children do enough moving around to feel physically content.

Young pupils need a change of pace intellectually as well as physically. The work in their room at times includes study by everybody, or silent reading. At other times, writing is the activity, or perhaps speaking and discussing occupies the group. The shift of study from one subject to another helps to keep pupils mentally sharp. Going to the computer room to work on reading or arithmetic represents a distinct change. The acquisition of new knowledge, being creative in artistic endeavors and strengthening one's physical skills makes for balance and alleviates fatigue.

11.

School goals and the programs designed to reach these goals are on the teachers' minds as they work with the pupils. These goal aren't secrets to be kept from the students. Pupils often set goals of their own, which makes the work challenging for everyone, including the teachers. Garden Hills motivates its pupils because it recognizes that each pupil is different — each is an individual.

The learning experiences are designed accordingly. Reading, arithmetic, and spelling are organized on an individual progress basis. A pupil progress plan utilizes end-of-level tests of skills in the basal readers, and end-of chapter tests in mathematics. As tests are completed they are sent to the computer center for grading. A profile of progress is provided in duplicate on each student — one for the parent and one for the teacher. Adjustments in instruction are based on results of the tests. When a student is not working up to potential, teacher and parents confer on how to help the pupil improve.

The 1985-1986 state program for the gifted, called "Challenge," enabled 48 Garden Hills pupils to spend additional time with the Challenge teacher over and above the work in their regular rooms.

Special education, which provides instruction for slow-learning or handicapped students, also plays an important role in diagnosing and dealing with individual differences. In 1985-1986 eleven pupils were receiving special instruction in speech and four in the area of learning disabilities.

Efforts of the staff to capitalize on events and activities outside the classroom in order to make classroom learning inside more meaningful, pay dividends. The Young Audiences programs, the culminating trip taken by the 5th grade each spring, the physical education sponsored May Day, the 4th grade field trip to learn about Atlanta and the RIF (Reading is Fundamental) auditorium program — often planned and implemented as outgrowths of classroom work — all provide incentives for development of skills in the classroom.

Dr. Benjamin Bloom, respected psychologist and researcher at University of Chicago, divides a human being's growth and development into two domains: cognitive and affective. The cognitive starts with skills — let's call them the Three R's — and moves through knowledge and generalizations into thinking and valuing. The affective, on the other hand, lies in the realm of feelings, attitudes and emotions, and embraces such characteristics as belief in self and respect for others.

Clearly the staff at Garden Hills has set goals that go way beyond the Three R's into the higher levels of cognitive and affective. In fact, some teachers strongly believe that the Three R's can be learned more effectively if they are taught in a setting of meaningful experiences which involve problem solving and thinking.

As one teacher put it, "If the children are relaxed, happy, and open with me, they are more apt to be receptive to whatever is going on in the room, whether from my demonstrating at the board or from a contribution by another student. If the involvement is relaxed, I think children learn better. If you are strict and inflexible, you don't get the lessons across as well."

Judging from prevailing standards at Garden Hills, it appears that its teachers have profited from their study of the Socratic method. Many times I noted while visiting classes that the teacher was consciously trying to talk less, to listen more and to ask questions instead of giving answers.

Also, feedback from teachers suggests that they feel they are accomplishing not one, but several goals when they incorporate reading, writing and speaking skills as a part of science and social studies teaching.

Principal Geren is a firm advocate of "teacher ownership," which means that teachers should confront their own problems and devise their own ways of solving them. When a teacher asks for help, Dr.Geren begins by asking questions to learn more about the problem. She never tells the teacher what the answer ought to be; rather, she helps the teacher arrive at an answer. The principal feels that she had her chance to "serve the ball" (or to give leadership) in coordinating the faculty and parent efforts as they worked to arrive at mutually agreed goals; now she wants staff members to find solutions on their own.

When a problem arises, therefore, Dr. Geren insists that the teacher "keep the ball in his or her court." Thus freed from the worry of carrying out someone else's orders, teachers can relax and concentrate on trying to accomplish on their own what everyone had previously agreed upon as the school's programs or objectives.

In spite of this independence, however, the principal and teachers share a team feeling and call the school "ours." It is also music to their ears when they hear pupils and parents call it "my" school. There is great pride here.

No doubt about it — Garden Hills classsrooms are good places to learn. Teachers care about the children, wanting them to develop to their greatest potential. Aware that the school alone cannot give pupils this opportunity, the staff has, therefore, entered into partnership with the home and community leaders. And the staff, parents, pupils and community leaders are grateful that they are part of a school that prepares students for challenging tasks — as stated in the formal words of the school's goals:

". . . . to perform as members of the family of mankind by showing responsibility and caring for people of cultures different from their own, acting as stewards of the earth and its resources, and practicing the skills needed to resolve differences by peaceful means."

Chapter Three

Twin Peaks Middle School: What Makes It One of the Best in the Nation?

1.

"I feel like the luckiest girl in the world today," began the 8th grader who had just been voted the most outstanding girl at Twin Peaks. Michelle H., speaking at a special ceremony for 8th graders who were now preparing to move on to high school, told how she grew in confidence and in achievement at Twin Peaks and thanked those who helped her along the way. "I am lucky not only because I received this reward," she said, "but because for the past three years I've been a part of one of the outstanding schools in America."

Unmistakable pride was evident on the faces of everyone present that morning, from the students to the teachers to the parents who had worked to make Twin Peaks one of the best middle schools in the country.

Twin Peaks is located in Poway, California, part of the Poway Unified School System, serving the communities of Poway, Rancho Penasquitos and Rancho Bernardo. Poway, once a small, quiet, rural town, has grown quickly in recent years and is now described as a bustling city. In spite of the large number of people who moved here to escape the fast pace of San Diego or other large cities, it is still regarded as a reasonably quiet, if not small, community.

Fewer than half its students come from the area immediately surrounding the downtown business district. The majority, about eighty percent, are from suburban homes of affluent, well-educated parents, and the remainder from homes where the income is less than fifty percent of the regional median income. Ninety percent of the students are white; ten percent are either black, Asian, Hispanic, or Native American.

Of the 93 staff adults at Twin Peaks, there are 61 professionals or "certified" personnel — 56 teachers, the principal, two assistant principals and two counselors. The remaining 32 are referred to as "classified" personnel — members of the office staff, custodians, teacher assistants and noon-duty supervisors. How these 93 adults work together was the single, most intriguing phenomenon that made me want to learn more about the school.

In 1985, the first year I visited Twin Peaks, I discovered that fourteen teachers and two classified workers were still on the staff who had been there since the school opened in 1971. And that 55 percent of the current faculty, considered "old-timers" although they are still far from middle-age, had been at the school at least nine of the past fourteen years.

It is this core of professionals, following eight years of something less than excellent administrative leadership, that welcomed the appointment of Judy Endeman as principal in 1979. They were particularly pleased with her drive, enthusiasm and creative bent of mind. Working with the school district's central office, Mrs. Endeman painstakingly recruited new personnel to complement the other loyal and committed staff members still at the school.

But what about the kids?

2.

The school day at Twin Peaks begins around 8:00 a.m. when 1,350 sixth, seventh and eighth graders swarm from school buses, a scene not much different from that repeated every morning, five days a week all over the country. As the young people mill about, I become aware of variations in their sizes and shapes — dramatic contrasts between prepubescent boys and already mature girls.

At 8:10, five minutes before classes start, the bell rings, compelling clusters of buddies to break up and head for their classrooms. At Twin Peaks, "classroom" may mean teaching space in any one of seven one-story buildings built around a quad or an adjoining elementary school or temporary movable units. Twin Peaks is already overcrowded, and I wonder how it will cope with increased enrollment projected for the years ahead.

Each school day is organized into eight periods (called "mods" from the term modular scheduling), a system that serves to make students' weekly classroom programs more flexible. In times past we used to call classroom periods "hours," even though no class ran the full sixty minutes. Of the eight mods into which the school day is divided, two are reserved for lunch. The remaining six periods or mods are reserved for basic subjects.

I was particularly impressed with the scheduling innovation of a reading break. Because Twin Peaks believes reading is important, its administrators have reserved time for a "reading break" which comes after the second lunch period and lasts 20 minutes. The reading break is a time for each

47

student and teacher too, to pick up a book, a magazine or newspaper and read quietly without interruption.

Another scheduling innovation is the concept of a rotating schedule. Traditionally, school schedules (and they persist in many schools in the United States) require a student to follow a rigid time table. The math class might be scheduled first thing in the morning everyday of the week; science might be fixed for the second period; and, say, English for the third period, and so on. This rigidity finds teachers and students running out of energy and concentration powers by the time they reach the last scheduled class of the day.

Under modular scheduling, however, a student's math class might come during the first mod (8:15 to 9:10 a.m.) on Mondays; during the last or eighth mod (10:55 to 2:45 p.m.) on Tuesdays; during the seventh mod (12:35 to 1:50 p.m.) on Wednesdays; during the third mod (10:10 to 11:00 a.m.) on Thursdays; and during the second mod (9:15 to 10:05 a.m.) on Fridays.

All of the students' basic classes are thus revolved according to a five-day cycle schedule posted for all students and teachers to follow. Teachers and students at Twin Peaks like the modular scheduling and find it easy to work with. No one seems to get mixed up.

As an observer of the rotating modular scheduling in action, I found that teachers and students like it especially because no class is scheduled for a first or last period more than one time each week. The moans and groans of teachers and students at being assigned a last period class are eliminated; as is the maneuvering that often occurs in order to draw a first period, which is often favored in school life.

It is during Mod 1, which runs 55 minutes, that staff members or a student reads aloud the daily bulletin. Students listen carefully to these announcements because nearly every day one or more items like these will concern them:

7th Grade Students: Tickets will go on sale this coming Monday for the end-of-the-year trip to the La Mesa Family Fun Center. Students who have met academic and citizenship requirements are invited to attend. Cost of ticket and transportation is $5.50.

Lost: Tan Purse. If found, return to office for reward.

8th Grade Boys and Girls: If you are planning to go out for any sports at Poway High next year, physicals will be given today and tomorrow from 6:00 p.m. until 8:00 p.m. You must sign up by this Thursday.

In addition to the inclusion of a reading break each day and the rotating mod scheduling, other basic indicators point to Twin Peaks as an exceptional school. These deal with test scores, parent judgments, teacher job satisfaction and student reactions.

Test scores – Students at Twin Peaks earn high achievement scores. For example, Comprehensive Tests of Basic Skills, nationally-used testing instruments, were given to all students at Twin Peaks in the spring of 1984. Scores made in reading, math and language were more than two grades higher than the national average. The average Twin Peaks student scored higher than eighty percent of middle school students throughout the country who took the tests.

In addition to high scores, 1987 tests confirmed that Twin Peaks students were continuing to increase the differences between their scores and the grade norms of students in general throughout the United States.

Parent judgments – One hundred and seven parents responded to a survey conducted in 1984 in the Poway schools. They were asked if they thought the school was doing a satisfactory job in basic skills; 96 said "yes." They were also asked if they thought the students liked school; 92 said they did.

Teacher job satisfaction – In a morale study conducted by a student in Claremont Graduate School, teacher job satisfaction at Twin Peaks was ranked from 3.5 to 4 on a 4-point scale, the highest of any school surveyed in this research. Two items that ranked highest among responses were "meaningful, worthwhile work," and "relations with other teachers" — meaning that Twin Peaks teachers were highly satisfied with their work and with their colleagues. These facts do not come as a surprise to me, for I arrived at the same conclusions from my observations: The teachers at Twin Peaks share a pride and enthusiasm; they cooperate instead of compete with one another; they are adept at recognizing problems which need to be solved and then get busy and solve them.

Student reactions – Not so long ago, a team of educators came to Twin Peaks to find out, among many other things, what its students think of their school. The team represented the Accrediting Commission for Secondary Schools of the Western Association of Schools and Colleges, a most prestigious group. In addition to many other questions the team asked students to tell what they thought about three programs. The questions were presented in this manner: "The math programs (or physical education, or music) that you have had are: excellent, good, average, poor, don't know. (Please underscore.)"

Fifty-nine percent said they thought their math program had been either excellent or good; only five percent "didn't know." Seventy-nine percent thought physical education was either excellent or good; only two percent said they didn't know. Results tabulated for music, however, are not valid indicators inasmuch as 48% replied it was excellent or good, but 36% said they didn't know — and for good reason, for most of these students did not take music.

49

Prior to Judy Endeman's arrival at Twin Peaks, things were not meshing well. At the end of the school year 1978-1979, parent participation was at low ebb. In addition, many key staff members felt programs were premature, and the result of insufficient planning. The school's principal requested a transfer to an elementary school and it was honored. To fill the vacancy, Mrs. Endeman was asked to tackle the job, and she accepted.

Mrs. Endeman's first year was a busy one. She knew from experience that parents instinctively become involved in their children's school when their children take part in band concert and talent show performances, art exhibits, etc. But she would need to learn more about the degree to which Twin Peaks parents and the surrounding community would want or would be able to become involved in school matters in general, such as in helping to assess and fill the school's many diverse needs.

Her first step was to send out a questionnaire to determine whether parents wanted to become more involved. Neighborhood coffee sessions were held with the principal and sometimes teachers in attendance. These informal gatherings encouraged parents to ask questions, and the principal was able to take the pulse of the community — to learn parental concerns and interests. Within a four-year period parents became deeply involved in many phases of school work.

Student participation in extra-class activities, too, rapidly accelerated. As of this writing, lineups include nineteen intramural boys' and girls' teams, plus sports competition in tournaments and all-star teams involving over two-thirds of the students. Seventy percent of the students are members of clubs whose interests range from Spanish, skiing, jazz band, honor society and "dungeons and dragons." "Spirit Day" activities on Fridays during lunch periods are exceedingly popular, while musical chairs and a game called "Coke bottle balance," provide fun not only for participants but also for those who watch.

The Associated Student Body (ASB) sponsors a student store, early evening dances and a student court. Students are voting members of the Parent-Teacher-Student Association (PTSA), the school site council, and The Gifted and Talented Education (GATE) Advisory Committee. This high degree of involvement led some students to provide me with this kind of feedback:

"We at Twin Peaks are fortunate to have such active, caring administrators . . . They care enough about students to sponsor special after-school clubs and activities . . . They always have a smile to share."

PTSA volunteers number over 600. They assemble newsletters, chaperone dances, help stage talent shows, coordinate events such as Picture Day, Pizza Day, band concert, teachers' luncheon and the eighth grade picnic.

Approximately sixty parents spend an hour or more weekly at the school working with students on a one-to-one basis while the teacher is occupied with other students. Additionally, 110 community volunteers help each week in classrooms, serve as resource speakers or appear as guests for the 6th and 7th grade career education program.

A well-planned project, devoted to setting goals for the school, was the vehicle that welded staff, parents and students in developing a quality learning program for Twin Peaks. At its heart was the School Site Council, organized in the fall of 1979 with parent, student and teacher members. A teacher began the venture by getting answers to a questionnaire presented to the staff and the student body. The next step then, in the fall of 1980, was to launch an effort to get the ideas of parents. Meetings were arranged in the homes of about 25 parents, selected so parents, staff members, and other citizens could walk to a neighbor's house. From these "brainstorming" meetings came a wealth of ideas for the school's roles and functions.

The resulting document, a creed if you will, consisted of a general statement of philosophy and goals, as well as ten specific goals. High on the list appeared the acknowledgement that the goal of any school must be to enable all students to develop to their potential in intellectual, emotional, ethical and physical growth. Also emphasized was the importance of school, home and community to work cooperatively. A sampling of three of the ten goals follows:

Communication and computation skills – Students will achieve potential in mastering the basic skills of learning . . . . listening, reading, writing, mathematics and critical thinking.

Self-concept development – Students will have a variety of successful experiences in the school so that positive self-acceptance occurs and self-confidence is increased.

Knowledge and appreciation of America's heritage – Students will understand the way the United States government works; will value the basic rights included in the Declaration of Independence, Bill of Rights and Constitution; and will appreciate the sacrifice of individuals who have contributed to the beginning and the continuance of our government.

What I find intriguing about this document is the use of the word *will* in each of its goals: "students *will* achieve their full potential," "students *will* have a variety of successful experiences," "students *will* understand the way . . . ." It is as though its writers did not intend to just *try* to achieve these results — there was a definite commitment that it *would be* done. Thus finding its direction, the faculty immediately began to assess where the school stood in relation to each of the goals and which programs needed to be changed to get closer to the established objectives.

At Twin Peaks, up-dating and up-grading of goals and programs never stops. Each year, goal statements are revised by the faculty and the site

51

committee as evaluation occurs and new developments are considered. This work takes thought, time and energy on the part of teachers and other staff members. Let's see how the process works.

Teachers, administrators and other staff members are in constant touch with each other on professional topics. First, there are the informal contacts, in the halls, in the lounge, at the lunch table. Many problems have been solved at these friendly encounters, many ideas and plans have sprung from such casual, but invaluable conversations.

On a more formal basis, there are the frequent faculty meetings, which are the core of teacher intercommunication and interaction. Prior to any faculty meeting, generally scheduled at 8 a.m., each teacher is given an agenda. Being informed ahead of time of the subjects to be discussed helps save time. Teachers who for any reason must miss a meeting, are given a copy of the agenda, with a note from the principal saying their input will be missed. The following day a copy of the minutes is given to each teacher.

The faculty meeting is one of a trio of elements at Twin Peaks that promotes intensive interaction and collaboration among the staff. The other two are (1) teacher teams and (2) the school's administrative cabinet.

Teacher teams – All teachers who have similar assignments make up one of several teacher teams. (Sixth grade basic education teachers serve on the same team; math teachers are a team; art teachers are another, etc.) Members of each team select a captain who is paid extra for this leadership role. Each captain coordinates teacher responsibility for carrying out policies and procedures; and also assumes personal responsibility for taking problems and issues raised by the teams to either the cabinet, the entire faculty or the principal, whichever is appropriate.

Teacher teams take up both short and long-range projects or problems. These may range from planning details for a class trip to formulating new curriculum ideas for the coming year which should be recommended to the cabinet.

Teacher team meetings are in no way routine. I dropped in on a 7th grade team meeting and found the principal there right in the midst of serious discussion. Mrs. Endeman said she thought that the basal reading program currently used by the school did not give opportunities for attaining some of the goals that the school believed to be important. She further suggested that some students in the basic teachers' groups might better be served by returning for a fifth hour when a teacher knowledgeable of their academic needs could help them.

She was interrupted by a teacher who spoke up vigorously in opposition to the idea. This threw the meeting open to a very lively discussion, but the principal was not upset. The result? A procedure was worked out whereby the problem would be examined further and reported back to the group.

The agenda for an 8th grade team meeting that I attended began with the showing of a film entitled, "Vocational Education — Is It for You?."

Then came ideas for next year's program to teach reading and writing, plans for a newsletter to parents and plans to find a speaker for the opening and benediction at 8th grade graduation ceremonies.

Cabinet meetings – Most decisions affecting the school emanate from the administrative cabinet made up of all team leaders. The principal is chairperson. Two assistant principals, two counselors, the principal's secretary, the librarian and an ASB advisor complete the cabinet. Because the cabinet is small, it is able to hammer out answers to questions and problems that have previously been discussed in faculty meetings. The cabinet picks up and moves ahead where the 60-plus faculty members leave off. During a five year period, cabinet action resulted in a new student discipline policy, a flexible schedule, study skill requirements and the modification and starting of several subject-matter courses. The cabinet also makes recommendations for administering a 1.7 million dollar personnel budget.

How the newly established reading lab is operated and staffed is a recent example of cabinet decision-making. The 6th grade class has use of the reading lab from seven to nine weeks during its sixth grade year. A basics teacher and the reading specialist who is in charge of the reading lab are both present during these sessions. In this way the basics teacher has an opportunity to learn procedures which may be incorporated in the reading instruction in the basic room. At the end of this period it is decided which students would profit from additional time in the reading lab during the 7th grade, and if necessary, into the 8th grade. Results to date substantiate the value of the reading lab in helping pupils overcome reading difficulties.

I attended one cabinet meeting at which smoking, alcohol and drug abuses were major agenda items. Four girls had violated the no-drinking regulation. A guidance counselor agreed to plan a series of meetings to be held with the girls' parents. An 8th grade teacher then announced the date of a day-long staff workshop which would feature San Diego Charger football team representatives who had volunteered their time to help schools with drug related problems.

The cabinet does not consider only items brought before it by teacher teams or the faculty as a whole — it often initiates setting new goals or modifying old ones. Taking advantage of these cabinet meetings to work closely with each of its members, the principal strives to help them sharpen their own problem-solving skills.

4.

If they are to capitalize on resources available to them, local schools must keep abreast of what is going on in the geographical areas of which they are a part. One way this is done each year at Twin Peaks is through distribution of a booklet entitled, "Superintendent's Goals," from the

Poway district superintendent's office, which is both a district progress report and a statement of educational goals.

Local schools must also look to their districts for guidance in working within district policies and procedures. Fortunately for Twin Peaks, the Poway School District plays a vital role in shaping the quality of the school's program, for the school would be hard put to achieve excellence without the teacher recruitment, curriculum and staff development and leadership supplied by the district.

And how could the school continue to grow without a fair budget, adequate buildings, materials and services — not to mention the invaluable backup provided by the district in spending $15 an hour for curriculum development (done on weekends and in the summer), plus payment of a stipend for team leaders? To name a few more, evaluation, bus transportation and scheduling are other areas benefiting from cooperation between Twin Peaks and the Poway district. What we really have here is a case of the district helping Twin Peaks, and Twin Peaks helping the district.

Poway teachers, for example, received a request from deputy superintendent Don Haught in March, 1985, for assistance in identifying goals for 1985-1986. Teachers were asked to react in writing on the quality and challenge of various textbooks and to tell whether they felt disruptions in their classrooms had been more or less than the year before.

They were also asked about homework policies and procedures — did they generate a noticeable increase or decrease in parent participation and support? And, perhaps most important of all, they were asked if higher level critical thinking skills and decision making in the classroom had increased, remained about the same or decreased. These ideas from Twin Peaks, when added to those from other local schools, helped the district formulate policies for the use of all schools.

But beyond its relationship with the district, a local school must cooperate with even larger, more powerful entities: the State of California, its Department of Education and the legislature. In recent years the tendency of this state has been to become deeply involved in decisions affecting local schools (i. e.; passage of Proposition 13 which severely curtailed school funds). Out of necessity, Twin Peaks staff members are learning to polish their lobbying skills.

One of their first attempts at influencing state officials — some would call it "arm-twisting" — resulted in the organization of a safari made up of two students, two parents, the principal from Twin Peaks, plus about 30 others from the Poway School System, all of whom converged on Sacramento to plead for more funds. As a result of this personal appeal, four legislators decided to visit the Twin Peaks campus to assess the school's needs. Net result? More money was earmarked for the state's schools, including the Poway District and Twin Peaks, and those who participated in the safari were convinced that they were instrumental in bringing about the change.

Over and above money, the state exercises control of schools in other ways. Textbook adoption is one — all schools must use California adopted textbooks. The state also maintains guidelines for each subject field. While local school districts and staffs of local schools do have a part in developing and modifying guidelines, most staff members find it difficult to feel a personal involvement in deciding curriculum at the state level. Because there are so many schools and so many teachers in California, only a few can be represented on the committees which finally present recommendations to the State Superintendent and State Board of Education.

The State of California has a testing program that directly influences every school and every classroom. State proficiency tests are given in grades 6 and 8. The California Assessment Program (CAP) is given again at the high school level. The results of these tests are crucial. Money coming from the state to the school district is granted in relation to the number of students who have improved on the CAP tests in contrast to the previous year.

Understandably, the subjects of academic testing and the values placed on scores are of great interest to lay people and professionals alike, but for the most part, California's Department of Education, has been looking for a middle road — one that holds out hope for low and middle achievers, as well as those with high scores, on educational quality indicators such as CAP and SAT (Student Achievement Tests).

The prevailing philosophy of the Twin Peaks staff about state testing programs extends far beyond their obligation to merely prepare students for test-taking.

5.

"Our job as teachers is to give students a good, sound education," one teacher told me. "The testing program is an administrative matter, and we fit in and cooperate with it, but we certainly don't let it control our teaching."

The staff at Twin Peaks evaluates, almost on a non-stop basis, what teachers are teaching and how students are learning. At times the staff seizes out-of-the ordinary opportunities for evaluation and improvement, such as the school's 1982-1983 self-study prepared in connection with application for accreditation by the Western Association of Schools and Colleges. Following a four-day visit to the school by a six-member team, the association granted Twin Peaks an eight-year accreditation — the longest period of approval given. Twin Peaks routinely utilizes the recommendations included in the accreditation report for program planning and improvement.

Furthermore, results of the most recent parent satisfaction survey, conducted by an outside agency every other year for the Poway School District, revealed definite upward trends district-wide in parent satisfaction over a six-year period (1978-1984). Prepared by the Mid-Continent Regional Education Laboratory, this report gave Twin Peaks other good news: The number of "yes" responses to two of eight categories charted for 1984 (basic skills and classroom instruction) showed 95 percent of the parents responding "yes."

Considering the variety and extent of methods used to evaluate its programs, Twin Peaks spares little effort or ingenuity. Failure to attain agreed upon goals signals staff members to go to work, and with the principal's leadership, to try to correct possible program weaknesses. Here is how one teacher viewed deficiencies detected in Twin Peaks programs: "In our regular curriculum we often do not let students make decisions that affect their lives. The basic education program does not provide many opportunities for students to be autonomous and then learn from their possible resulting mistakes.

"Historically, the tendency has been to neglect this area of a student's education. How can we expect young people, when they are with a group of their peers on a weekend, to have had enough practice in decision-making?"

My conclusion, after close observation, is that about 75% of the Twin Peaks staff do not regard (nor treat) goals, program and evaluation as separate elements in the operation of the school. They are warp and woof of a total process of planning and follow-through. And I believe that this is one of the major reasons for the school's ability to sustain its high standings.

Most of us acknowledge the importance of knowing what direction we want to go before we set out, and we also know it's a good idea to check from time to time to see if we are still on course and that we stay there. This kind of planning is relatively simple when it pertains to one person, but how can this idea be applied to a school — where many people are involved, say 93?

At Twin Peaks it is done with a staff of professionals who generate a climate in which it is considered normal and natural to be checking on oneself or in conversation with colleagues about whether what is happening is sound or debating if they have the evidence to know they are on the right track. Each year is a whole new ball game, with new players. What's more, a whole year of developments outside the school causes the staff to take a fresh look at what's being done in the classrooms and on the campus.

6.

It has been wisely said that "they who dare to teach must never cease to learn," meaning, of course, that teachers must continue their education on and off the job. This process, called inservice education or staff development, is promoted through seminars, workshops and the use of consultants. However it is done, it costs money. In many districts, administrators first see how much money they have for staff development and then provide the programs.

Twin Peaks reverses the process in deciding staff development activities. First administrators define what kind of help teachers need and then worry about where the money will come from to pay for the seminars, workshops and lectures required for the staff. If the money is not immediately available, the staff starts to look for it and usually ends up finding it — somewhere. The principal and some of the staff are known for their grant-applying ability. Everyone, for the most part, keeps a close eye on county, state and federal sources of money which may be available, upon application, to local schools. Business, industry, service clubs and foundations are not overlooked.

Often a decision to launch a new teaching venture is reached by a teacher as a result of his or her own self evaluation. "I feel an ownership of my room, and I am responsible that my students make good," a teacher explained. "To do this I must have elbow room to organize the room in a manner that makes me feel comfortable and competent."

Principal Judy Endeman believes that any staff development program must consist of a good balance between on-site, after-school, released-time training and off-site conference attendance. But where does the money come from for such staff development activities?

Sometimes it comes from the state, as it did during 1980-1984 when a California staff development grant funded a major portion of the Twin Peaks program involving such goals as improving school climate, developing positive discipline among students, promoting computer literacy and improving supervision. Funds for sending teachers to state and national conferences for further instruction in subject fields sometimes comes from the State Compensatory Education and the Gifted and Talented Education (GATE) programs. In 1982-1983, teachers from Twin Peaks staff attended the State Reading Conference and the National Science Educators Conference.

Teachers also like the clinical teaching workshop sessions conducted each year as part of the Poway Professional Development Program (PPDP). This program, approved in 1982 by the school district for certified staff of all Poway schools, covers learning theories, lesson design, classroom management and questioning techniques. When teachers attended the three full-day seminars in 1984-1985 prior to the opening of school in the fall, they were paid $50 a day. It is estimated that from the beginning of the PPDP in 1982-83 through 1985-1986, three-fourths of the teachers at Twin Peaks attended these seminars, an indication of how highly they are valued.

"Project Impact," the type of workshop attended by teachers on released time, emphasizes that teaching competence requires the infusion of training into existing programs of mathematics, reading and language arts.

"Project SMILE" (Supportive Methods for Improving Learning Effectiveness) is the name given to another staff development project. Intro-

57

duced in 1980 at Twin Peaks by a San Diego State University professor, SMILE workshop sessions helped teachers identify and experiment with the use of certain subtle, but vital classroom strategies which are known to improve the learning environment.

The first such strategy is called physical proximity. Inasmuch as isolation is sometimes known to cause distress in students, researchers say it is important that a teacher move from behind the desk, circulate around the room and be in close contact with the students. According to these researchers, a hand on the shoulder, maintaining eye level with the student, even occasionally a shoulder bump, are simple but important gestures to help students overcome the feeling of isolation and to sense support from their teacher.

Another strategy is called validating — meaning to "give positive reinforcement or assurance." Some experts propose that the teacher's grade book contain a column for entering a checkmark whenever the teacher had "validated" a particular student or given positive assurance that something had been done well. The teacher can then see who had been neglected or ignored and plan to reinforce any forgotten students with some form of personal acknowledgement.

These techniques are based on the philosophy that all students have potential for good and that there will be signs of positive behavior, providing you look for them. Twin Peaks teachers believe this theory and try to discover which methods work for each student.

Twin Peaks also provides opportunities for teachers to upgrade their work through summer school attendance. A math teacher told me about a mathematics course he had taken, requiring two summer sessions, at a San Diego area university. He described the sessions as a program to rejuvenate teachers, and spoke highly of it. Other teachers confirm the value of similar staff learning experiences in a broad variety of disciplines.

One good way to promote professional skills is to provide opportunities for individual teachers to work on the curriculum — to help update subject matter; revise teacher guides; recommend new content in science, math or history for inclusion in teaching programs. One administrator explained why the district should utilize teachers in doing curriculum work. He said that teachers are "out where the action is" and therefore will develop curriculum materials that are practical and useful. He also said that relying on teachers for curriculum development is more economical than employing additional central office staff for this purpose, or going out of the district to employ consultants. One Poway central office staff member estimated that the system was spending $150,000 a year for staff program planning and development. He further thought that the district leads the county in determining how much of its financial resources go into curriculum work.

Principal Judy Endeman also takes part in self-improvement activities. For several summers she attended week-long workshops sponsored by the

Kettering Foundation's Institute for the Development of Educational Activities (IDEA). Recognized throughout the country for its high quality, IDEA workshops enable participants to explore new teaching and administrative methods and to meet new professional friends.

7.

"Parents have become a real force in the life of Twin Peaks," a teacher told me. "We now have more than 600 parent members of PTSA (Parent Teacher Student Association), and they contribute much to making our school one of the best."

It is evident that there is good rapport between staff and parents. When parents come into a classroom, the discussion does not come to a sudden halt — the climate is one of openness and honesty. A parent told me that she considered it a privilege to take part in the work of the school, especially when she felt she had had an active role in making a particular project a success.

Parents are most often enthusiastic about their school. I heard many complimentary stories about the extra efforts of many teachers to provide exceptional learning experiences — like the physical ed instructor, at Twin Peaks about fifteen years, who has given up his winter vacations for more than ten years to take students, and often their families, on ski trips. One mother is convinced these outings helped her once-shy daughter to become more outgoing, to acquire new friends and to feel, for the first time, a part of the school.

Parents serve on three school committees: the already mentioned School Cite Council which helps to assess successes or failures in attainment of projected school goals, gifted students' advisory committee and State Compensatory Education. This last school committee is responsible for offering programs in which students who are physically, emotionally or educationally handicapped can succeed.

Probably every public school in the nation has some form of parent/teacher association, and it is no coincidence that the overall quality of a school is frequently related to the degree of participation and cooperation bestowed upon it by its own PTA or PTSA. Notice that at Twin Peaks "S," for students, has been added to the customary "P" for parents and "T" for teachers when referring to this association.

What the PTSA contributes to this school is almost endless, and the following rundown will in no way, I am sure, tell the entire story, but it is a beginning.

Besides chaperoning parties and 8th grade dances and providing transportation for field trips and athletic events, parents sponsor a teacher appreciation luncheon each year and plan a variety of occasions to thank other volunteers like the Grandpeople who give so freely of their time. Parents also help in the library, referee games and train themselves to become teachers in the Junior Great Books program. Add to those activities family ski trips and bicycle rides, and it's not hard to understand what makes this PTSA special.

Money-raising demands a lot of the association's time and energy. The PTSA executive committee (with representatives from students, parents and staff) decides what school programs need funds to supplement the regular school budget, and then decides how to raise the money. One of their most highly successful money-raising events is the annual variety talent show, which runs for three successive evenings.

As part of a county-wide program, businesses and industries work closely with schools. To illustrate, TRW, a major high-tech industry in the district, has adopted Twin Peaks. TRW contributes much to enrich the school's programs — presenting U. S. savings bonds as Science Fair awards; providing resource speakers for classrooms; organizing a conference for girls entitled "Expanding Your Horizons"; and encouraging field trips to its facilities. Especially rewarding, I was told, was a breakfast carrying the theme that "Tomorrow Is Truly Taking Place Today," held in the spring of 1985, aimed at bringing staff members up to date on technological developments.

But Twin Peaks also does things for TRW. The school's music director, for example, composed a march for TRW to use in its company ceremonies; and the school band has played at TRW open houses.

As part of her effort to involve the community, Mrs. Endeman initiated the school's Grandpeople Program. She asked me to coordinate it; as a resident of the area, I could not refuse. The Grandpeople Program, she explained, would open the school to citizens who do not have students in the district by inviting them to volunteer their services in whatever capacity they desired in areas where the school most needed help. Over 100 people participate in the program in many ways — providing one-to-one experience to students, giving classroom talks on foreign lands or contributing personal insights to career awareness classes.

I believe the Grandpeople Program adds much to the educational process at Twin Peaks, but it took a confident, imaginative leader and staff not only to want it, but to make it work. It challenges citizens to come to learn about school firsthand.

Unanimously, participating oldsters report a revitalization in their lives as a result of their work with schools. They speak of the joy they derive from being allowed to come into the classrooms, to work with children in meaningful pursuits, to know that their knowledge of the past is respected and can in some way contribute to the enrichment of today's youth. One of the Grandpeople recently expressed her feelings in these words: "Our contact with the children keeps us young in spirit, young at heart, keeps our minds alert and clicking, keeps our sense of humor and laughter in our repertoire. Thank you for letting us share in the world of today."

Another volunteer, who is in his 80s, gets satisfaction from helping 6th grade pupils with their lessons. It is hard to say who benefits most from these associations — the young or the older folks. But if you ever had the opportunity to observe a 6th grade boy, at the close of school, carrying art equipment in one hand and guiding an older gentleman to a waiting car at the curb, you would have no difficulty understanding the value of these relationships as they developed during the Grandpeople program.

An innovative idea brought by Principal Endeman from an educational conference she attended bears the name "Mystery Guest." This plan invites citizens outside the school to come to class to discuss their careers. The program begins with a question and answer period similar to the old TV quiz game, "What's My Line?", wherein students try first to guess what the guest "does" or "did." The students love it. By the time they've identified the guest's present or previous vocation, the students are ready to listen intently to the guest's comments about careers and the world of work.

While the school receives direct and indirect help from the community, it also reciprocates by helping the community. Students respond to the community by contributing food and money to worthy causes and frequently visit retirement homes. Many of the school's staff members participate in community endeavors, including principal Judy Endeman who has been active on the board of directors of the Poway Boys and Girls Club, and teachers who have served on the Rancho Bernardo Recreation Council and on the Little League board. Staff members welcome invitations to attend civic gatherings and are often invited to speak before the Women's Club, Soroptimists, Kiwanis and other groups.

Twin Peaks believes that nothing takes the place of direct contact between teacher and parent. Especially useful, I believe, is the school's traditional "open house." Many parents will recall "open house" as the time when most of them were first introduced to their children's teachers, when all the classrooms were spruced up and students outdid themselves with special exhibits to decorate the blackboards and walls, making certain the student authors' or artists' signatures were large enough to be read from the back of the room!

Open House at Twin Peaks sometimes takes another route — one called "Shadow A Student." This is great fun because it permits a parent to follow his or her child for half a day in a spontaneous, unrehearsed, normal classroom atmosphere. Later I will describe my experiences while shadowing a 6th, a 7th, and an 8th grader.

Parents, teachers and school officials contact through a variety of written material. When a teacher wants to compliment a student, for example, one-page messages called "Ram Grams" are sent home with the student.

Publications are numerous and well prepared. *The Twin Peaks Ram*, a student newspaper, and *Reflections*, a student literary publication, keep parents and students informed on school news and student achievements. The PTSA also publishes a monthly newsletter.

Three district publications report happenings in all Poway schools. *The Morning After*, appears the day after a board meeting, describing what happened the night before. The January 5, 1987, issue in my possession listed gifts made to schools in the district the previous month — including two to Twin Peaks: an astromicrowave from the Twin Peaks ASB student store and $339 from the Kiwanis Club of Los Rancheros for the purchase of software for the reading lab. *School News In Brief* and *Kaleidoscope* publicize achievements of schools throughout the system.

8.

My observation during the two years I visited Twin Peaks convinced me that students welcomed involvement in school governance and in extracurricular activities. This attitude was based on the students' realistic appraisal of their school. On one occasion, a class of 7th graders were invited to tell what they liked or disliked about their school, and they responded with 190 "good things" as opposed to only 55 "bad things." Said one student, "What I think is good about Twin Peaks is the ASB (Associated Student Body). It is a very good idea to let us feel what it's like to make decisions."

Many of the responses involved complaints about fighting, smoking, inadequate and cramped facilities, too much homework, too short breaks. Students said that if they had their "druthers," they would rather have classes start earlier in the day, a cleaner campus, less stringent school rules, better food, freedom to eat lunch at a location of their own choosing, less homework and a larger campus. Responses didn't change much when the same questions were presented to an 8th grade basic education class. Fifty-nine students there listed 197 positive replies as contrasted to 84 negative. Satisfaction with their school remained dominant.

Nonetheless, if these 8th graders had their way, they would improve the school's food, elicit more school spirit, start earlier in the day, allow more lunch time, do away with the reading break, have cleaner lunch tables, permit more freedom, have more time between classes and have a new gym. Two students thought they shouldn't have to pay to ride the bus, the lockers were too small and there was too much discipline.

With very few exceptions, committees mentioned throughout this examination of Twin Peaks lean heavily on student involvement. Students have representatives with voting membership in PTSA, the Site Committee and the GATE committee.

The PTSA executive committee gives the student representative an opportunity to work on problems (involving the three key school groups: parents, staff and students), many of which relate to both out-of-class and in-class experiences. GATE is state-mandated and provides an excellent opportunity for student representatives to help challenge the more gifted learners.

As student representative during 1984-1985 on the site committee (also state-mandated), Paige S. shared her thoughts about this assignment: "My job, basically, was to present the views of the students and to bring up subjects that the students thought needed improvement. I was also expected to give an ASB report on recent and upcoming activities."

"I appreciated the way members of the board made me feel comfortable and respected — that what I had to say was important."

Participation in the Associated Student Body (ASB) is probably the students' first exposure to operating within a formal, democratically structured organization with specific goals in mind. ASB's four top positions — president, vice-president, treasurer and secretary — are elected by the student body. Serving on the board is considered a privilege and honor, inasmuch as its members assume responsibilities for many of the activities that bind together the students, staff and community.

The school capitalizes on this activity to help students understand nominating procedures in our adult society. In the spring of 1985 Judy Endeman opened meetings for grades 6 and 7 by reminding them that in a few years they would be adults, expected to make decisions about their local community, state and the United States. And she appealed to them to be serious and thoughtful as they participated in the ASB election. "Your experiences now are very important in getting you ready for tomorrow," she said.

What follows is not much different from the usual fanfare preceding other significant elections: Rules are established and either followed or challenged; caucuses flourish between ballots; the pep band hypes up the electorate, candidates expound with impassioned appeals from the platform. Once elected, the ASB cabinet meets at least once a week. To observe the ASB teacher sponsor as he guides various groups through informal discussions, raising questions to help students come to grips with problems, and then to have it all fall into proper place, is to watch a master group-leader in action. Not an easy task this — getting young people to tackle even so simple an event as a barbecue dance, for instance, with full responsibility for planning publicity, scheduling, invitations, choice of bands for music and getting chaperones.

I suppose it would be pleasant if we could operate our schools without having to worry about money-raising pursuits, but on the other hand, how would our young people learn one of the facts of life — that there is no such thing as a free lunch? And so it is that at Twin Peaks fund raising is an ever-constant, important adjunct to book learning.

Need a wrestling mat? More musical instruments? Additional equipment and materials for the career center? Invariably, the ASB will have a hand in coming to the rescue. ASB was instrumental in raising $6700 for the Camperships Program for 6th grade Outdoor Education, Twin Peaks' largest money-raising venture in the early 1980s.

In the spring of 1985 I attended a money-raising planning meeting called by a guidance counselor. First, he asked 6th grade officers for assistance in finding a way to raise the $7500 required to complete purchase of the equipment and materials still needed for the newly established career center. Since career education was beginning in the 6th grade, the staff decided this would make a good beginning project for 6th graders. What evolved was a Jog-A-Thon, with donations from parents and neighbors to be made on the basis of the number of laps each student would run on the school marathon track. First prize for the student running the most laps was a Schwinn bicyle; second prize earned $25 in a savings account, and any student running more than six laps received a turtleneck T-shirt.

The basic room group that earned the most money would be treated to a Padre baseball game. One day a Twin Peaks bulletin announced the winners:

> "Congratulations to the 6th grade basic ed class for raising a record $390.58 for the career center and winning the trip to the Padre baseball game. The 6th grade assembly will be held today at 1:25 in the quad to award prizes for the Jog-A-Thon."

At the community level ASB has raised money for asthma research through a Bike-A-Thon, and for the Salvation Army in its Adopt-a-Family Christmas Drive. The school also sponsors an annual canned food drive that netted over 3500 canned food items distributed at Thanskgiving time. Seventeen classes adopted families for the holidays and purchased gifts for family members. Visits are made to the Twin Peaks Retirement Home during the holidays. The students join with the community and parents on Earth Day in a campus beautification project. The list goes on.

Twin Peaks staff believes that no sharp line exists between planning some "out-of-classroom" activities and "in-classroom" learning. Orchestra and modern science classes meet before school in the morning. GATE has after-school classes and social events as well as being a part of classroom experiences.

Music plays a big role in the Twin Peaks student development process, and a program that once consisted of two bands has now grown to five involving 370 students. Band classes meet daily. Members also meet before school many times during the year to prepare for the music department's fifteen annual Jazz Band concerts. Off campus the music department performs for such organizations as the Lions Club and the county fair; the top three bands play in local festivals each year.

Vocal music and drama groups are also active. Parents and the community are invited to attend performances such as "Sound of Music" and "Carousel." Participation in these presentations, however, is not limited to those in music classes but is open to anyone in school who wishes to "try out." When the cast needs a more mature person for a particular role, alumni are sought at Poway High School.

Having previously examined the value of campus publications in keeping students, staff, and parents informed, we cannot ignore their preparation, or production, as a valuable process in promoting the study of journalism. The school newspaper *Twin Peaks Ram* and the annual *Reflections* are, of course, class projects, but because of the time involved in researching, writing, editing, printing and distribution, they also come under the heading of extra-class activities.

These publications are very popular. As I thumb through them, it becomes evident why. The issues of the *Ram* before me contain jokes, an interview with the school principal, plans of the chapter of the California Scholastic Federation, an article on the cross country track team, a trivia test, a puzzle, an article on the most popular music records of the day, interviews with students and a staff member on "What is your favorite TV show?" In this instance, the staff member interviewed is the head of the maintenance department — surely a reflection of students' respect for those who serve to keep the school's plant and grounds clean and safe.

Every student's picture appears in the 98-page annual *Reflections*. Baby pictures are numerous and always good for a laugh. Twelve pages show students busy at their elective courses. Staff pictures consist of one posed and one candid shot for each staff member. Students working on the *Annual* take all the photographs with the exception of the group class pictures. All of which adds up to another student favorite — undoubtedly because it becomes a personal collectible — a book filled with pictures and containing a minimum of words.

How is it possible to distinguish between learning for the sake of learning and learning because it's fun, when events — planned or otherwise — are inextricably interwoven? Take the 6th grade Olympics for instance, a joint effort conducted each spring by the physical education department and 6th grade basic teachers. Each basic group selects a foreign country that it wishes to represent and appears at the Olympics site dressed in appropriate native costume for the country selected. Some of the teachers also dress for the occasion. During the track events, often lasting all day, a number of basic groups manage booths where they sell food and other articles.

Another event that binds students together is the intellectual competition contest, "Academic Bowl," in which basic rooms vie with each other or the faculty just as contestants compete in the familiar TV game show classic, "Jeopardy!" Anyone who has ever watched this popular program can testify to the enthusiasm that such competition creates — especially when you can beat the teacher.

Initiated by Tom Cruz, an assistant principal, the program begins with a series of questions that have been developed by the staff; answers are contained in the books used in regular courses. Sixth grade basic rooms compete with one another, as do 7th and 8th grade rooms. A round robin tournament scheduled for each grade level results in final matches being held in the evening before hundreds of parents and classmates. Also during this tournament, one of the student winners competes with the faculty — to the delight of the onlooking students. In the event that I observed, the 8th grade team won over the faculty which, not surprisingly, the faculty took in stride.

In the written application for national recognition, Twin Peaks staff listed fifteen clubs which, when added to nineteen intramural teams for boys and girls, involved more than seventy percent of the student body. This is a remarkable testimony to the extent of student participation. In checking these fifteen clubs, I found nearly all of them closely related to classroom subjects: Spanish, the classics, rocketry, manufacturing enterprises, home economics, drama and music.

Trust in People (TIP), student store and honor society relate more to the school itself. Fishing and a game called "Dungeons and Dragons" seem to be the only two that are unrelated to a school subject.

"Spirit Day," along with the two clubs just mentioned, has all the earmarks of something done just for fun. An assistant principal started Spirit Day when he came to Twin Peaks in 1980. It is celebrated every Friday — related, I am sure, to the day of the week that has traditionally become "T.G.I.F. (Thank God It's Friday) Day" in the work-a-day, study-a-day world. This activity occurs once during each lunch period and not only draws a large number of participants but a larger audience. When I asked the assistant principal the purpose of Spirit Day, he acknowledged that "kids will do better in the classroom if they sometimes have fun at school."

Every autumn, at the start of school, the entire Spirit Day schedule for each Friday of the school year is posted, listing from 35 to 40 different contests, one to be held each Friday of the school season. Take your pick: you've got to excel at something! How about musical chairs, pickle-eating, flying paper airplanes, ping-pong shot-put, popcorn stringing, peanut and spoon races, or three-legged races?

One Friday I observed a tug of war — any basic room could enter the contest with ten boys and ten girls. The 6th grade champion room tugged against the 7th with the winner taking on the 8th. All of this is able to happen in ten minutes because many students are enlisted as helpers. Student Dave M. describes the Twin Peaks 500, one of the Spirit Day activities:

"Every year just a few weeks before school gets out, the annual Twin Peaks 500 is held. The 500 is a miniature car race in which the cars are designed and made by students in the Industrial Arts class. The cars are made out of small blocks of wood. Every student gets a chance to participate in the race of his own class. Then the first, second and third class winners in each class go on to the semester finals and then to the actual Twin Peaks 500. The track that the races are held on was constructed by the Industrial

Arts teacher around 1977 or 1978. I think the Twin Peaks 500 is a tremendous asset because the students can take a real sense of pride in something they created all by themselves.''

Added to the prestige of winning any of the weekly Spirit Day events is the thrill of seeing the names of contest winners published in the *Poway Chieftain*, the local newspaper.

9.

An 8th grade basic ed class was asked what it thought of the reward and penalty systems at Twin Peaks. Of a total of 55 replies, 39 commented on rewards and 16 on penalties. Ten students thought TIP (Trust in People) was a sound recognition for good behavior. Student court, harbor cruise and Disneyland trips were mentioned by five or more as proper rewards. Seven commented on the application of Saturday school attendance as a penalty and four on detention. "The staff has set up a number of incentives for good behavior and good grades," one student observed. "TIP allows many rewards for good conduct such as picnics, ice cream fetes and such. There is also the honor society for students who get good grades.''

"There are many punishments from detention to Saturday school," she added. "Another way of getting justice is through the student court. I am the court clerk and I have noticed a big change in the number of people who break the rules. The reason for this is that the students who are tried become embarrassed in front of their peers. I am proud to be a student at Twin Peaks. The rewards and punishments are terrific. I wouldn't change a thing!''

"I think the disciplinary system is very good," another student agreed. "If you litter on campus, you have to spend a lunch Mod picking up trash on the quad. I got caught littering once last year and I had to clean up the quad — I was so embarrassed I never littered again.''

"Twin Peaks punishes those people who don't do well in citizenship," a third student spoke up during one discussion of rewards and penalties. "If a student gets a U (unsatisfactory) in citizenship, he is put on a list of students to be watched. If he gets another U, he becomes ineligible for trips like Disneyland and the harbor cruise.

"If someone is caught smoking, he or she is transferred to another middle school. My parents told me that when they were my age, there were just warnings when you did bad things and there weren't any rewards for trying to be good. I'm glad our school has both.''

One day I loaned a dime to a student in the 7th grade basic room. She came to me a few days later to return it. I regarded this as a reassuring sign of how most of the students at Twin Peaks regard responsibility and honesty.

Student membership in TIP is cherished at Twin Peaks because those who qualify by earning E's for excellence in deportment are granted a variety of school privileges. They form separate lunch and bus boarding lines. They are the first to be dismissed from a classroom at the end of a day. They are honored at special assemblies, including an annual hot dog picnic at Poway Lake.

When I asked a staff member the rationale upon which these privileges were based, she explained that in order to make good behavior popular, "you must provide rewards that mean something to the students — not what adults would consider sound."

The feeling among faculty members is that good discipline emanates from a positive atmosphere established by a majority of the students — making it desirable for others to follow suit. If the situation is reversed, students who create discipline problems often become heroes in the student body.

Letting students know when they have done a good job is considered by the school staff to be a prime motivator. For example, one warm spring day the entire Twin Peaks student body of over 1300, plus the adjoining elementary school of some 400 pupils, gathered on the grass in the quad to take part in a ceremony sponsored by TRW. At the close of the assembly, Mrs. Endeman complimented the students on their good behavior and received loud applause when she announced that free ice cream cones would be available at the lunch period the next day — compliments of the PTSA. I commented to one of the teachers that the students certainly behaved well. He nodded in agreement but hastened to add that while most of them were orderly, "two students in my group pulled up grass and threw it at each other. I am going to see them right away and give them detention points."

Recognition for good student behavior receives as much, if not more, attention. At an awards assembly, I observed many examples of honors bestowed on students who excelled in one area or another. Included were winners of the 6th grade spelling bee, students with perfect attendance, those who completed second year of Spanish while still in middle school, yhose who gained outstanding achievement in science and five boys for their skillful craftmanship exhibited at the County Fair.

In each of these instances the teacher for the particular subject made the awards. Noteworthy students in home economics, drama and music were also recognized by their teachers. If the looks on their faces meant anything, students in the audience displayed genuine pride as their classmates marched to the stage to receive their recongitions.

But students aren't only awarded at assemblies for outstanding efforts or accomplishments. Teachers also follow a practice of presenting an appropriately worded certificate to students whenever they have done something special. Four typical certificates contain these messages:

"Your behavior has been right on target. This award presented
to _____."
(Teacher's name and date)

"Super-citizen award presented to _____."
(Teacher's name and date)

" _____: "Your work has been dynamite in _____."
(This particular certificate contains a lively drawing to illustrate the power of "dynamite.")
(Teacher's name and date)

"Smooth sailing ahead for _____."
(Teacher's name and date)

There is also a certificate reserved especially for a student who occasionally misbehaves but seems to be on the way to improved behavior.

Admittedly, teachers sometimes have to look hard and long to find something worth rewarding. One day a teacher discovered that a girl in her class was listening intently, contrary to her usual demeanor, showed interest in what was going on and displayed a pleasant smile for the entire period. The teacher rewarded her with one of the "Smooth sailing ahead for _____." certificates.

Teachers are vigilant in monitoring students who waste time and misbehave. They are, for the most part, responsible for discipline in their rooms, although they may sometimes turn to assistant principals for help. Usually, however, teachers hold afternoon conferences with the offending students at which time the teacher decides what penalty should be meted out. Some teachers require that students stay after school, but when this happens, additional school work is not likely to be assigned because teachers do not want students to associate forced learning as appropriate punishment for misdemeanors.

Not infrequently, behavioral problems parallel learning problems, and when this occurs, parents are called to the school for conferences. In serious cases, parents, basic teachers counselors, and all other teachers of the pupils in question meet in an effort to work out a plan to help the students overcome their difficulties.

I visited a Saturday school, one of the penalties, near the end of the school year. In one classroom there were 28 students and one teacher who had been employed to supervise the activity. During the four hours they spent in that room, students were asked to think through their difficulties and to propose ways they might be overcome. A list of their offenses revealed that seven had been sent to the Saturday school for truancy; six for rudeness and/or disruptions; five for fighting; three for obscene remarks; two for incomplete work; and one each for smoking, chewing tobacco, damaging school property, missing a teacher's assigned detention or throwing rocks.

Later I asked an assistant principal if I could talk with some of the students who had been in Saturday school. The first boy I spoke with told me that he had been having trouble for some time at home with his parents, but that problem had now cleared up. He also said he was sick of getting into trouble because he lost too many friends by not being able to "pal" around

69

with them on Saturdays. So he decided to try to cooperate on the school's terms and felt good about his decision. He agreed that the school did need harsh discipline measures, and as far as he was concerned, "Saturday school was OK."

The second student, a boy who had spent two terms in the 7th grade, admitted that he had cut school many times the year before and had been tardy a lot. He said that although he felt he and his teacher were getting along better this year, the real reason he had decided to "shape up" and stay clear of Saturday school was due to a visit home by his older brother who was in the Air Force. His brother laid it on the line: "You can't be a jet pilot without good grades." This advice impressed the younger boy because he realized he wasn't going to go anywhere in life "if he didn't cut out the monkey business."

Suspensions or transfers, considered by students to be more severe forms of penalty than Saturday school, numbered 22 at Twin Peaks during 1983-1984. In the minds of most students, almost nothing can be worse than being excluded from your peers. Transfer means that you are assigned to Meadowbrook or Black Mountain, the other two middle schools in the Poway district. Suspension means not being allowed to attend regular classes but still being assigned to some room at school, or it may mean being sent home. There were no expulsions at Twin Peaks that school year.

Student court, initiated in the fall of 1984-1985, enforces rules on campus and at the same time teaches students about the legal world from both sides of the bench. Sponsored by an assistant principal, the court includes judges, attorneys, bailiffs and court clerks, all of whom are chosen from the student body on the basis of academic standings and good citizenship.

Teachers who observe misdemeanors on campus (fighting, using foul language or other violations of good behavior) can issue student citations. One copy of the citation goes to the student and one to the court clerks. A student who believes another student has damaged his personal property can also file a complaint. Students choose their own attorneys.

The court hearing I attended took two sessions to resolve. A student had accused another of taking his pizza from his plate at lunchtime! The accused party initially pleaded innocence, but before the end of the second hearing and on the advice of his attorney, he confessed his guilt and was duly sentenced.

The students take their judicial responsibilities seriously. The fifty or more students I observed in the audience at the hearing remained orderly. At the close of the session, I asked several students, privately, what they thought of the student court. Each told me that a student considered punishment by his peers to be more severe than by a faculty member — an interesting observation, in my opinion, inasmuch as the penalties imposed by students in student court closely follow those imposed by staff members!

Two years later, when I inquired again about student court, I learned it was even more active and even better received than before.

A 6th grader who had been at Twin Peaks for about six months talked with me about the school's other systems of recognitions and penalties. "In middle school you can have punishment or fun," she said. "It just depends on how you act. If you're bad and don't turn in your work, you'll get an F, get detention or get Saturday school. But if you're good and turn in your work, you'll be on the honor roll which means you get all A's and B's on your report card. Plus you will be in Trust in People. Once you are in TIP you can do special things, like leave class first or get in a special line for cafeteria or bus. Personally, I'd rather go for the good things."

One teacher expressed the opinion that the school's disciplinary process would benefit from greater consistency. "We on the staff — and I mean all of us from the custodian to the noon duty lunch supervisors, teachers and the principal — have to be more consistent about what we expect in campus behavior," she said. "Students behave differently in front of different individuals because they understand what certain staff members expect and how far they can go. And the kids will play the game as long as we remain inconsistent. I might be idealistic — maybe we can never reach 100% consistency because we have such varying personalities — but I think it is something we ought to strive for."

Twin Peaks welcomes its students at the beginning of each school year with an inviting brochure, advising them that their job for the next nine and a half months is to perform to the best of their abilities, follow school rules and behave in a manner that neither disrupts nor distracts from learning tasks. "Together we can make our school and our nation stronger," Principal Endeman promises on the first page of a recent leaflet.

This message to students appears in another part of the booklet: "You forfeit your chance for life at its fullest when you withhold your best effort in learning. When you give only the minimum to learning, you receive only the minimum in return . . . . When you work to your full capacity, you can hope to attain the knowledge and skills that will enable you to create your future and control your destiny. If you do not, you will have your future thrust upon you by others. Take hold of your life, apply your gifts and talents, work with dedication and self-discipline."

The leaflet contains a section on student conduct — seven guidelines and eighteen rules and regulations in all — spelling out what students can expect if these rules are violated and what they need to do to become part of a good school.

On the subject of maintaining discipline, a teacher commented that although the issue of student conduct is important, "with students such as we have, high standards are not difficult to maintain." And an assistant principal, in discussing the relationship between staff expectations and student performance, said that "we have to believe that the students are capable of

whatever we expect of them. When we say, 'We know you can do it —
therefore we expect it — ' they believe you.''

Every fall discipline is an item on the planning agenda. After deciding
what went well and what did not the year before, the staff maps out
changes in plans in an effort to make the coming year more successful.

Poway School District officials back up the individual schools on developing and maintaining good student discipline. Written district policies
make it easy for staffs and parents alike to understand and follow the rules.
The consensus at Twin Peaks prevails that the surest way to guarantee good
adult citizenship is to develop good adolescent citizenship.

10.

I am going back to school again. I am going to learn first hand what it's
like to be a student at Twin Peaks during the latter half of the 1980s. My
plan is to follow, one by one, three students as they go from class to class. I
decided to ''shadow'' Chris L. on my first day of this venture. He is a tall,
thin, young man, wearing a serious facial expression, shuffling slightly as
he walks. Our first class is held in the computer room where he is scheduled to spend a total of six weeks learning computer skills under the leadership of the school's computer specialist. This instructor has help from a
volunteer parent who prepared for her role as a computer resource person
by taking an evening computer course.

Amazing things begin to happen as the assistant demonstrates how it is
possible to create images on the computer screen by manipulating the small
rectangular instrument she holds in her hand. Circles, dots and straight
lines miraculously become trees complete with brown bark and green
leaves. Later, the teacher challenges students to construct, in the middle of
the screen, a red block with a dot above it. Not all students are able to do
this at first, but eventually they succeed.

At 10:00 a.m. Chris and I go to his basic education room to take on the
subject of arithmetic. Nineteen students are present; five out with flu and
colds. Five students leave the room — four to advanced math classes elsewhere, and one to a remedial class. The remaining fourteen students are divided into two groups called the ''Parallelograms'' and ''Pentagons.'' The
Parallelograms are instructed to take a test and then to work on a math puzzle. The Pentagons, arranged in a semi-circle at the other side of the room,
review their homework with the teacher, everyone obviously trying to keep
their voices low so as not to disturb the Parallelograms while they are taking their test. They also get back the tests they took the day before and discuss their errors with the teacher. I was impressed to learn that students
could raise their already-graded test results by correcting their mistakes.

I also observed that practice exercises, named and designed to make
problems fun to solve, motivated students to try to do better. They espe-

cially seemed to enjoy "playing" a game called "Music to Your Ears," involving the reduction of fractions to their simplest form. The exercise begins by having students cross out each fraction already at its lowest term and also the letter that appears in front of the fraction. The remaining letters, they find, will spell out the words of a new song. As an extension of this exercise, students are encouraged to make up their own tunes. The teacher speaks softly. Students who want to contribute an idea or answer raise a thumb instead of a hand. (Is nothing sacred anymore?) Pupils on both sides of the room work seriously and diligently, including Chris L., the young man I am shadowing.

The teacher does not use a text in math, preferring instead to follow the Poway curriculum guide. But the closet in her room overflows with an intriguing collection of materials for use in keeping her students challenged. She strives to individualize each pupil's work and appears to group pupils only when they share common difficulties. She charts graphs of the levels of attainment of each of her students (determined by test results) in math and language arts skills, broken down into areas of specific difficulties — such as addition, subtraction, multiplication, division, decimals, fractions and measurements for math.

At 10:55, in the same room, Chris and I move on to reading, at which time youngsters again separate into groups — one group working with the teacher on a novel and the others, staying at their desks to work unassisted on reading skills such as decoding more difficult or longer words. A few students do not settle down; in a quiet but firm way the teacher reminds them that time on task is important: "Let's go to work."

Before volunteering to read aloud, the group working with the teacher on the novel, *The Indian in the Cupboard*, turns in its homework assignment. One large boy appears reluctant to read aloud. The teacher tells him he doesn't have to, but asks, "Can your arm be twisted?" He smiles and begins to read. My presence, for the most part, goes unnoticed, but occasionally a student and I exchange smiles.

The pupils at their desks, without reminder from their teacher, work until they finish the chapter (about twenty minutes before the end of the period) and are asked to answer several questions. At the end of the period, Chris hands the teacher a card upon which she makes notes about his work up to this point. Chris tells me later that this card keeps his mother up to date on the progress of his study habits and behavior.

At 11:40 Chris and I go to a special education class where the teacher, with one assistant, works with six pupils to help them improve their ability to concentrate. I learn from the teacher that her pupils possess the promise of significant improvement. Students here, all of whom are at least 1.5 years below grade level in one or more subjects and need remedial work, are assigned to these special classes when it is determined that they suffer "deficiencies" in reading.

Following a warm-up vocabulary workout, the class turns to spelling. Chris L. keeps busy up until ten minutes before the hour is over when he begins to stare at the clock. I learn that Chris has been in Special Education since 1980 — that he had suffered medical problems leading to a lengthy hospital confinement — and because of his illnesses, he got a lot of attention which undoubtedly delayed his natural ability to learn on his own.

After lunch, at 1:20, we return to the 6th grade basic education room where everyone (and I do mean everyone, including the teacher) immediately opens books of their choice and begins to read. There are no interruptions until the bell rings twenty minutes later.

At 1:40, the teacher announces that, as she had promised, she is going to introduce a three-dimensional way to draw, inasmuch as most of the students, up to now, had only drawn in two dimensions. On the blackboard she proceeds slowly and precisely to draw a building with two visible sides, explaining how to arrive at appropriate starting points and to make the right linear connections which willl depict a building in perspective.

This was not meant to be an exercise in copying what the teacher put on the board — she encourages them to be innovative. Pupils were asked to decide on their own where to place their horizons and where the observer will be standing in the illustration. Consequently they end up with a great variety of designs: tall and short buildings, narrow and wide structures.

I conclude that this teacher is able to sustain maximum student interest and cooperation as the result of her system of placing students into subgroups in terms of their individual needs, with one small group working independently while she works with the other. The classroom environment is relaxed. There is little apparent wasted time. The teacher likes to leave students with something to think about. "If you like doing this," she tells a student at the end of the art period, "you might consider taking drafting classes."

Chris and I go to physical education, our last period for the day. Here I learn that each P. E. teacher has an assigned group organized on a co-ed basis. Groups usually average about thirty but for some sports the classes are as large as sixty. Calisthenics kick off each period as a warm-up activity. Nearly every conceiveable sport is offered: interscholastic sports involve soccer, football, track, volleyball and cross-country; while intramural sports, occurring during the school day, include indoor soccer, racquet ball and aerobics. A bus leaves at 4:30 to take home students who are involved in after-school sports.

Twin Peaks participates in the President's physical fitness program which involves testing three times a year. Junior Olympics, billed as an "internationally flavored" event, are held annually.

On the day I visited, cross-country was on the schedule. Pupils lined up for the trek that would take them around the track and the playing field, totalling a run slightly over a mile. A timer clicked off running times as pupils reached the finish line, and a teacher recorded the time in the classbook. When the front runner approached the finish line, we were all surprised to see that a wisp of a girl came in first!

Physical education in schools that I have observed over the years, in many instances, emerges as a time when both pupils and teachers seemed to take it easy. But my exposure to the program at Twin Peaks tells me that at this school a serious set of objectives exists for the promotion of health and creative use of leisure time.

Chris L. and I now part company. I had a good time and I wonder if he did too.

I have just been promoted to the 7th grade. This "shadow" day I am going to follow Danyel D. Her basic education class begins with a test for those pupils who did not get a perfect score on the previous day's weekly spelling list of twenty words. Since Danyel had gotten a perfect score, she is excused from taking the test. Students are next asked to define four words. Danyel finished her definitions early and begins to tap nervously on her desk. Her teacher smiles at her and shakes her head.

A warm-up test containing eight sentences asks students to identify verbs and to tell whether their tenses are past, present or future. A second part of the test involves punctuation of sentences appearing on the blackboard. Next there is an eighteen-sentence verbal phrase exercise (underline each auxiliary, write verb phrase on the line after each sentence, etc.). During the last fifteen minutes of the period pupils read news items, including one about the weather.

Danyel and I go next to her physical education class which will feature a softball game since this is Friday, the day normally reserved for intramural sports. It proves to be Danyel's shining hour; she thrives on P. E. and today she is the star. The sound of a bell (without which no school could possibly operate) twelve minutes before the end of the period, signals everyone that it is shower time.

We went to Danyel's math class where we found a girl distributing a warm-up test. She offered me a copy of the questions. Danyel is very nervous — crumpling and crackling a piece of paper. She couldn't keep her mind on her work and made paper airplanes after finishing the practice exercise. Homework, I am told, is assigned on a four-day basis — Monday through Thursday. Seventh and 8th grade pupils are placed in math classes by achievement levels, not because they happen to be in the 7th or 8th grade. (Math I indicates comprehension ability below 7th grade; Math II, 7th grade; Math III, 8th grade; Math IV, pre-algebra; Math V, algebra; and Math VI, beyond algebra).

Basic class, including the 20-minute reading break, is next on our schedule. The teacher reads definitions and asks pupils to write the word fitting each definition. Most of the period is spent taking tests and doing exercises with not much time left over for oral expression or discussions — probably because it is near the end of the semester. The last part of the period is devoted to reading and discussing three paragraphs about Cicero.

Period 8 takes us into a typing class. Danyel enjoys typing and today she is allowed to use an electric typewriter. I am told that a teacher's assistant is recording the grades for this class, and that 8th graders are allowed to apply for these types of teaching assistant jobs.

Pupils normally elect to take typing five times a week for one semester although they can take an additional semester if they choose. Two computers are available for word processing. Students type newspaper articles that have been written by the school newspaper staff — certainly a more interesting approach to practicing typing than the endless pages of dull, unrelated words and subjects that I recall offered in most typing textbooks. For the last twenty minutes on Friday, the teacher allows boys to cluster around one computer to play games on it and the girls on the second.

As we walk from one class to another, Danyel and I have an opportunity to visit. "I like typing very much," she tells me, and has elected it for a second semester. She is also trying to learn how to use the word processor and has a typewriter at home which she often uses. She admits that although she really doesn't like reading very much, she thinks she improved some after attending the reading lab in the 7th grade.

It is interesting to note that as students move up the grade ladder at Twin Peaks they spend less time in basic ed classes. For example, in the 7th and 8th grades, they have their basic teacher for only two periods instead of five as in the 6th grade.

When I asked the 25 students in the 7th grade basic ed class in which Danyel was enrolled to react to the question, "What do you like most and least about your classroom?" the answers were so varied that no definite pattern could be established. However, I think the comments of one student provide a fairly accurate assessment of how most of the students regard their school: "I think overall that Twin Peaks is a great school. We have our strong points and our weak points. But I think kids here basically like it and don't really mind learning because we learn the basics plus a lot of other things."

"We have a good physical education program. I love it and I think most others do too. The teachers and the program push us to do our best. My running has really improved this year, as well as some other basic physical exercises. I have fun too. But there are some kids that really don't like P.E. I can understand that. I don't think they should be pushed too hard. In time they will come around. If not, that shouldn't be held against them — it's just not in their nature. I was like that once too."

"We have a super academic program with A-1 teachers who are ready to help you learn. Some people might not like school, but that should not hold others up who do. We are still growing and improving — but aren't we always?"

David B., a student in an 8th grade basic group, and I pair up for my final "shadow" journey. Somewhere along the way, I asked David if he would write up for me how he feels about his classes.

"It is Monday," he begins. "My first Mod is band. I feel it is misnamed because 'band' is a class where you learn to play music. Here we are pushed way beyond our playing and learning limits. I feel that instead of 'band,' it should be called 'music appreciation and learning how to do it right.' I know that's awfully long but at Twin Peaks it shouldn't just be called 'band.'"

"Mod 2 is basic education. The education I'm getting from this teacher, probably one of the best, isn't basic at all. I think of it as an 'anything' Mod — we may have a test on World War II, a debate on world political leaders or something as simple as a lesson on verbs, nouns and adjectives."

"In my opinion, Mod 3, Physical Education," David continues, "is one of the best in the state. Many of our students take the wide variety of classes offered (from basketball to something as obscure as golf) for granted."

"Mods 4 and 5 — math — people groan at the thought of math but it is almost fun here. Teachers treat us as equals and not kids. They talk to us as adults and explain things in ways we can relate with and don't use a bunch of terms that people don't even use any more."

"Mod 6. There isn't much I can say about lunch except that it's probably everyone's favorite 'class.'"

"As a teacher's assistant, I spend Mod 7 running errands, grading papers, or recording grades — anything the teacher doesn't want to do or doesn't have time to do."

"Back to basic ed for Mod 8, American History hour. Our teacher uses a style that can cram twenty years into our heads in a day and we aren't even aware of it. Most of us learn even if we don't want to."

"Well, that's how my Monday goes. I think Twin Peaks is one of the best middle schools in our area — not because of facilities or because it's only fifteen years old, but because of the programs and the people in the school who are teaching us."

It pays to take a closer look at David's comments about his participation in the school band, described as his first Mod on Monday. Poway parents insist that their district schools produce the very best bands possible. And while school people concur with citizens about this goal, they also want everyone to recognize that students must necessarily sacrifice some other school experiences while they are in band. For example, 6th grade band students have only four-fifths as much time in school to do their work as those not in band.

Band consists of five levels of proficiency: advanced (of which David is a member), concert, intermediate, cadet and beginning. I wanted to watch them at work so one morning I arrived at the band room fifteen minutes before school started. Half of the class was already there tuning up instruments; and by the time the tardy bell rang, the instructor had already passed out music folders! I was moved by the young musicians' rapt attention as they strove to synchronize their efforts through the several compositions rendered during the available time.

In David's Mod 2 (8th grade basic ed), the teacher and students seemed to be in agreement on what was to be done from the time the bell rang until the dismissal signal. I asked one pupil how this is accomplished, and she explained that it was possible because of the way their work weeks are planned, that contrary to convention, "our work week starts on Thursday rather than Monday. I feel that this way is better because you really have seven days to work on homework rather than five."

"On Thursday we get an assignment sheet with the four basic education subjects (English, literature, spelling and history) printed on them. Filling out an assignment sheet is a good way to keep track of the weekly assignments and the dates they are due."

"About three to four days a week, for about the first ten minutes of the first Mod, we write our thoughts or feelings into a journal which is confidential and treated seriously by the students. I think it is good because it gets your feelings onto paper."

"Often on Monday an essay is due when we can express our views on different problems in society such as drug and alcohol abuse, world political dilemmas, etc. Then we stand before the class and read our essays. Sometimes this can be embarrassing but it is a good speaking experience."

"This year in literature we read two good books: *Tom Sawyer* and *Hiroshima*. We also read other stories, plays and poems from a literature book. At the end of each chapter or story, we discuss about ten related questions."

"This has been a very educational year for me — I have learned a great deal in my basic education class."

There was one interruption during the 2nd period when two students from another 8th grade room came to the classroom to distribute a questionnaire on teenage morals, as part of a class research survey experiment. Students were invited to answer the questions, at home if they desired, and to return the forms the next day. Some of the questions . . . .

Do you feel that men and women are equal?

Is drinking OK?

Is it OK to use drugs?

Do your parents help you and listen to what you have to say?

Do you think that teenagers of today and those of thirty years ago have similar problems?

In his third period, Physical Education, David B. wasted no time. After calisthenics, he jogged around the half-mile track — both of which appear to be class requirements. Then, because of his P. E. schedule, he moved on to a basketball court to learn more about zone defense.

Fourth period found David in his math class — level 6 — advanced algebra. The teacher worked with the students on dependent and independent variables, using an overhead projector which, he said, helped him to keep eye contact with his students at all times.

After lunch David and I go to a classroom where the teacher is leading an elective class in writing for 7th and 8th graders. David leaves me on my own while he, in his role as assistant to the teacher, runs errands to the main office and library. Following the customary 20-minute reading break, students received directions for submitting poems for a poetry book. How adjectives enable a reader to visualize what the writer is saying was discussed and then students went to work on a writing assignment. Finally, a three-minute brainstorming session generated a lot of talk among students about what they expected to do during the summer months which were not far away.

At 2:40 David and I return to his basic room to hear a student's report on South Africa, touching off a lively debate about American companies that invest in that country, currently torn by racial tension. Preparation for high school enrollment occupies the class next, with the teacher stressing the importance of planning. As the students scanned the booklet, "Futures — Making High School Count," the teacher confers with individual students at his desk.

Each student in the class completes a weekly progress report which, everyone hopes, will end up at home. We used to call them 'report cards' — remember? But in this instance the student does the evaluating. The report lists nineteen phases of student work to be evaluated. They are measured by a zero for unsatisfactory, two for satisfactory and four for above average. The weekly grades in English, spelling, literature and history are part of the progress report. Comments such as "comes prepared with materials," "is responsible and organized," "respects rights and property of others," "assignment not complete," are graded.

Space is provided on the report for parents to raise questions or offer suggestions; the signed report is then returned by the student to the school.

11.

So ended my shadowing ventures at Twin Peaks. But my interest in the students continued almost insatiably. Even before the shadowing experiences, and certainly after, I kept directing all sorts of questions to the students.

When I asked a group of 8th grade students how they felt about their school experiences, one student volunteered: "In the 6th grade I learned about the early Indian civilizations, Incas, Aztecs and Mayas. I learned

79

about the four types of sentences: declarative, imperative, interrogative and exclamatory. In the 7th grade I learned about the Renaissance, the Middle Ages and life in Europe from very early times to modern times.''

"This year, my 8th grade, I think I have learned the most. I learned how the first people came to America. And about the Revolutionary War, the Constitution, the Civil War, World War I, the Great Depression, the Spanish-American War, World War II and many other important events in America's history. I have also learned all of the parts of speech. I have read *Tom Sawyer* and *Hiroshima* and written reports on them. Every week we learn thirty new spelling words and have a test on them. I think the opportunities at Twin Peaks are fantastic.''

Another student, Lisa A., told me that Twin Peaks makes learning fun for the student, something I heard many times over. "Teachers with a good sense of humor relieve tension in the classroom — it makes it easier to learn. Some of my teachers allow us to carry on interesting activities, like debates in the classroom, so we learn while exchanging ideas with other students. A wide variety of clubs and activities also makes learning easier and more fun.''

Lisa doesn't think Twin Peaks has many negative things about it. "I can't really think of anything wrong or that needs improvement. You should leave school feeling refreshed — and I do.''

Student Monica D. says that "most of our teachers keep the class under control, making it nice all around. But I do wish some teachers wouldn't get so uptight about people who don't learn as quickly as others. I wish they wouldn't get mad at students who give wrong answers. When teachers get up tight, it makes us uncomfortable and we freeze — we don't want to ask or answer questions.''

Bryan H. likes the general appearance of the school. "The grounds are clean, and the equipment is kept up and classrooms are neat and tidy. Kids enjoy coming to a neat, clean classroom, not a dirty, messy place. I wish some teachers would make their classes more fun and be a little more lenient. The general atmosphere should be relaxed; you can't learn when you're worried about getting into trouble.''

I am convinced that one of the major reasons Twin Peaks students score high on tests is that the work for each individual is tailor-made as much as possible. This means, of course, that each student, challenged on the basis of his or her strengths, sees sense in what they are doing and are asked to do.

Efforts made in the classroom to individualize work pay off. Grouping of students into small groups for certain projects — allowing teachers to work with individual students while others study on their own — contributes to the establishment of good rapport between pupils and teachers.

Rationale for such grouping makes sense. Not everyone in a class is, or operates on, the same wave length, and there is no dictum that requires all pupils to work on the same subject at the same time. Having a portion of the class study independently in one part of the room while the remainder of the class interacts with the teacher in another part of the room serves several purposes — the most obvious being, of course, that more ground can be covered in this manner. Furthermore, the teacher can give more individualized instruction since, at least for part of the period, she is working directly with fewer students.

Another advantage of grouping, for purposes of individualizing instruction to fit the needs of students, is that it allows them to proceed from where they are in achievement — thereby reducing the possibility of getting lost (because their comprehension may be below the level of most of the class or bored because they have already learned what is being taught). The mathematics program, which is arranged by subject levels without reference to grades, seems to be working very well.

The state funded program, GATE, also provides groups more freedom to decide where and what they will study by clustering students who are eligible for the gifted and talented program. On a sunny day, for instance, it is not unusual to see three or four GATE groups doing their work while sitting under shade trees on the quad. We may even discern discussions being led by one of the students.

I have talked of the Grandpeople and parent volunteer programs before, but it is virtually impossible to over-emphasize the valuable contributions volunteering adults can make to individual pupils. As coordinator of the Grandpeople program, I knew of a boy who had severe discipline problems. Because reading gave him a lot of trouble, he was assigned to the reading lab. There a senior citizen worked with him under the supervision of the reading specialist and lab director. Amazingly, after only a few weeks, the boy not only quit misbehaving but also started to overcome his reading troubles. A teacher who had been following this case told me that the boy's mother worked, and had little time for him — his stepfather had no interest in him — he was literally starving to death for some kind of positive relationship with a caring adult. As time went on, the youngster spoke often of the senior citizen who took an interest in him. Someone liked him. Someone cared about him. Someone had time for him.

Let me underscore: Twin Peaks goes to great lengths to tailor-make educational programs for each individual. The reading and math labs are good examples, and the special education program is still another example. Faculty members are especially alert to the needs of newly-arrived students from Italy, Mexico, Iran, Japan, Pakistan and other countries.

One teacher told me that some of these immigrant students have strong academic skills, while others are functionally illiterate. ''I remember Pedro and Lupe who, never having been in school before, blew into the room like tumbleweeds. Pedro came to love poetry and books. He learned to play chess and won second place in a school tournament.'' And even though

81

students enter the program with vastly different skills, she says, "they all share mutual needs of acceptance, freedom to make mistakes and opportunity to grow in an unhurried atmosphere."

It would be impossible for a young person attending Twin Peaks not to find something of high interest in the school's elaborate menu of electives: a rich arts program, shop courses, typing and foreign language, fine arts, music and drama and a physical education offering that embraces almost any sport a student might want to become more serious about later in life.

Learning, researchers tell us, can be measured immediately and more directly by looking at student behavior in the classroom than by analyzing grades of achievement tests. Based on this research, ALT (Academic Learning Time) emphasizes the need to utilize every minute of classroom time for learning, and Twin Peaks does its level best to do just that — through an effective plan by which both the teacher and parent keep track of how well a student is doing. One teacher explained how the system works in his classes: "At the start of the school year I require students to have a 3-ring binder notebook which they can divide into separate sections for each subject. In the front of the notebook I suggest the addition of an enclosed plastic holder for pens and pencils. Since implementing this policy I find that students are much more consistent in terms of classroom preparation by having the needed paper, pencils, etc., and in turning in their work."

"In addition, the school prints yellow weekly assignment sheets which contain the calendar for the month on the reverse side. I hand these out to students at the start of each week. There is a place to record the homework or assignment for each subject for each day of the week. There is also space on the calendar to record long-range assignments and homework assignments for the next day which are copied from my chalkboard. Students insert these sheets in the front of their notebook to remind them of all work. This system helps students organize their various assignments on a daily basis."

A student agrees that "my notebook helps organize my stuff. My different classes are separated and I don't lose my homework and other things. I put phone numbers and my schedule on the front and I clean it out every month to keep it organized."

"Warmup" and "sponge" activities (not to be confused with physical exercise or bathing) are responsible for much of the school's success in making good use of every available learning minute. Warmup activities are provided at the beginning of a period when teachers have before-class responsibilities to discharge and cannot start to work with the entire class immediately after the bell rings. So pre-planned practice exercises put the pupils to work on their own until the teacher is able to start the class rolling.

Principal Judy Endeman stresses that having materials available for practice work at the beginning of periods is at the heart of the warmup program. When she came to Twin Peaks in 1979 she brought the warmup idea with her which soon caught on, and teachers were subsequently employed to write suitable materials during the summer. "We knew that if we taught fractions to students in September," she said, "they would forget them by the end of the school year unless they had practice along the way."

Because the warmup idea seemed to work so well, the same principle was directed toward end-of-the-period time when some students have finished the prescribed work while others haven't. These activities were called "sponge."

"The object is not to waste learning time," Mrs. Endeman emphasizes, "but to use the first five minutes as well as the last five minutes of a learning period."

Sometimes I can't help but compare Twin Peaks teachers to athletes going into a game — players who remember what they agreed to in strategy meetings and then resolve to accomplish as a team what they set out to do. But they also adhere to the philosophy that they have to be free to be themselves — relaxed and natural, in order to be most effective. They are not encouraged to adhere to a particular style of teaching. At one extreme there are teachers who never seem to have to become strict disciplinarians; their students just naturally tend to business. At the other extreme there are teachers who automatically raise their voices as they become sterner.

Because teachers often relate to each other in their team planning, they have many opportunities to learn from each other. The growth — the changes that occur in individual teachers from year to year as they work with students and relate to their colleagues — is both noticeable and admirable.

The principal and assistant principals who supervise the teachers believe that after they have done their best to help them through individual conferences and group meetings, staff members should be respected as mature thinking adults who probably know more about what should be done in their classrooms than any administrator. The administrative people at Twin Peaks understand this. Consequently, they spend most of their time working with staff members on projects, not as their bosses but as fellow workers.

CHAPTER FOUR

McCluer North High School:
Profile of a Superior Urban School

1.

Bill Hampton, principal of McCluer North High School, spoke slowly, reflecting on events that affected his life. "I was born in southeast Missouri, in very poor farm country. My father was in the 7th grade when both of his parents became sick with scarlet fever, and he had to leave school to work the family farm. He was the oldest of seven children, forced at the age of 12 to quit school and become a farm worker. Although he had the help of an uncle, he pretty much ran the farm as any 12-year old might have done.

"Later we moved to the city where my father became a sheetmetal worker. Although he didn't have a formal education, my father was smart and bright mechanically. He came home from work one day, when I was about 14, and proudly announced that he had been promoted to superintendent of a local warehouse that stocked metal. It was the high spot in his life.

"But the joy didn't last very long: three months later he became ill again, requiring him to look for another job that would be less strenuous. It was then that he realilzed that his limited educational background was preventing him from functioning effectively. Written and oral communications gave him a hard time. Although I was only 13 or 14 at the time, I empathized with my father, because I was sure he would have been able to fulfill his potential had he had the educational opportunity.

"So here I am a principal — seeing poor families send their children to school. Many of our black children are from a poor community and their parents haven't had the opportunity to go to school, either. And that's a major obstacle to the fulfillment of their dreams, too."

84

"If it weren't for public schools, I couldn't have gone to school at all. If it weren't for public schools, my father wouldn't have even gotten to the 7th grade and my mother wouldn't have finished high school. Now you can understand my deep commitment to public schools where people of limited means are presented with the opportunity to overcome enormous obstacles. And if that can't be true in a democratic society, we're in trouble — terrible trouble."

"A school isn't only a building," he said, "it's an expression of beliefs and attitudes about ourselves and the generation of young people for whom it is planned. In its silent language of space, scale and shape, the structure stands for what we are, what we think of ourselves and what we believe we can become. Whether we are planning programs or buildings, we cannot afford to guide our decisions on anything less than our deepest faith in people."

And so it is that the scale and shape of McCluer North High School tell us more than how many square feet it contains. In that silent language of space that Dr. Hampton spoke of, we learn not only what the people who dedicate their lives to teaching think of themselves, but how they regard the students who have been entrusted to them for guidance.

Approaching McCluer North from any direction, the beauty of the building, framed by rolling hills, well-trimmed lawns and colorful shrubbery, causes the observer to take a deep breath, perhaps even to say, "I sure wish some of the schools I went to had looked like this!"

Seeing the structure and its surroundings for the first time, a visitor senses a feeling of openness — difficult to explain. The red brick high school building, irregular in shape, stands two stories tall on the south and four stories high on the north, suggesting versatility, energy and strength. Adjacent to the campus are the school district's central offices and the Florissant Civic Center.

McCluer North's interior is as impressive as its exterior. Dramatic architectural design features an open two-story concourse on the first floor, adjacent to the cafeteria. A spacious library with wide, colorful halls houses 20,000 books on the second floor. Bordering the cafeteria area is the Activity Center, a favorite spot for students to mill around and visit with friends when time permits. Above the Activity Center and next to the library are the advisory facilities, which I shall discuss in the section devoted to this unique student service.

Dr. Hampton explained that a major consideration for placing the school in a setting removed from other buildings and providing open spaces within, was to avoid, as much as possible, potential distractions. Another was his conviction that high school aged students can best be helped to prepare for adult living by keeping the school environment apart from possible negative influences of metropolitan city life. He is, however, a firm advocate of students going into the community to participate in various projects

85

and programs as learning experiences. So it helps that McLuer North is not too far removed from community and industrial life. It is located in suburban northwest St. Louis County, Missouri, next to the airport and such industrial giants as McDonnell-Douglas and Emerson Electric.

McCluer North is a 9-12 grade comprehensive senior high school with an enrollment of 1800. Its student body is 77 percent white, 21 percent black and 2 percent Asian and Hispanic. Pupils come primarily from low and middle income homes. Sixteen percent of the homes are considered "very low income," — making students from these homes eligible for the school's free or reduced-price lunch program. McCluer North is one of three high schools in the Ferguson-Florissant School district, which also includes eighteen elementary schools and three junior high schools, with a combined enrollment of 12,000.

McCluer North opened its doors in 1971. Four years later, in a move to modify racial imbalance in the schools and with integration as his constitutional aim, a federal judge ordered two adjacent school districts — Kinloch and Berkeley — to incorporate into one Ferguson-Florissant district. As a result, all of Kinloch Senior High School's 600 students descended on McCluer North. Problem No. 1.

Subsequently, between 1976 and 1984, enrollment declined from 3200 to 1800. Problem No. 2.

And if that wasn't enough to make a principal wonder why he ever chose "principalling" as a profession, the district asked McCluer North in 1983-1884 to become a four-year high school and to absorb all ninth grade students from its three junior high schools. Problem No. 3.

These were formidable problems. Any one of them could have caused a school to falter and even to close its doors. But McCluer North not only overcame them but managed to emerge as one of the finest urban schools in the country. Luckily, it had the right leadership for the job, the support of parents and the community, the cooperation of the faculty and the involvement of students. The survival and success of McCluer North has to be attributed to everyone who joined forces to create this extraordinary secondary school.

But how can we really measure a school's success? By examining what students end up doing after they leave school? Counting awards and recognitions? Analyzing test scores?

Of the students who graduated from McCluer North in the spring of 1983, fifty percent went to a four-year college or university, twenty percent enrolled in a community college, three percent enrolled in vocational training, 3 percent enlisted in the military, 10 percent found full-time employment and fourteen percent part-time employment.

Twenty-six McCluer North students won awards in 26 academic competitions during the years 1981-1984. Eighteen made it to the National Merit Program finals. Early in 1984 in a scholarquiz competition, called

Telequiz, for St. Louis area city and county schools, McCluer North won first place. Nine students earned special awards from such organizations as the National Chemistry Association, Harvard Book Award and National Council of Teachers of English Writing Award.

The school's Community Outreach Program was rated one of the nation's top ten in a study conducted by the University of Wisconsin. The school's yearbook, *Polaris*, and its newspaper, *Stargazer*, received high ratings from the National Scholastic Press Association.

Behind these significant student accomplishments, positive forces were at work: Strong partnerships between the school, homes and the community; and down-to-earth staff planning with consistent follow-up to guarantee the translation of plans into action. Longtime service of key professionals adds another plus, with fifty-two staff members — 54% — having been in the school since 1973-1974, McCluer North's first year as a complete three-year senior high school. Under the leadership and coordination talents of Bill Hampton, the school's first principal, this initial group of teachers not only "stuck with" the school through traumatic changes, but strengthened it as well.

2.

Satisfactory completion of studies at McCluer North earns one of two diplomas: a comprehensive diploma or a scholastic advanced work diploma.

To graduate with a comprehensive diploma, students must complete a minimum program consisting of three credits in English, three in social studies, two in math, two in science, two in physical education and health, one in fine arts and one in practical arts. In addition, they must earn eight elective credits.

To satisfy the requirements for a scholastic advanced work diploma, students must have four credits in English, three in social studies, two in math, two in science, two in a foreign language or three credits of a concentration in either art, business, drama, home economics, journalism or industrial education. Approximately one-fourth of the students qualify for the scholastic diploma by taking advanced work, also referred to as "honors."

The daily schedule contains six periods. Normally all students take subjects every period; there is no regular study period. Students are expected to study within their 55-minute classes and at home. School starts at 8:15 a.m. and regular classes are over at 2:45 in the afternoon, but the campus is often alive until sundown with students participating in extra activities. In the evening, many students head back to school for a variety of meetings.

3.

In a school as large as McCluer North, it would be easy for the individual student to get lost in the crowd, but this does not happen here, due in large measure to its advisory program which is designed to guarantee students adequate personal attention. In summary, the advisory system provides a plan for the parents of a student, a staff member and the involved student to work together in determining what the student should strive to do in his or her four years. An advisor works with the same students for four years. Each year, therefore, only one fourth of the students are new to the advisor.

Every staff member at McCluer North is both an advisor and a teacher. Advisors also become members of advisory teams, consisting of five or six teachers who share information and ideas from each other as well as students and parents. To carry forward the advisory concept, teachers confer with individual students or with groups of students, each week for a total of two hours, during which time substitute teachers take over their regular classes.

When 9th grade students or transfers first come to McCluer North, they and their parents confer with their designated advisors as the first step in making educational plans. One decision the student has to make is which of the two certificates to work toward — the comprehensive graduation or scholastic certificate. Next, a four-year program is outlined to reflect post-high school plans and interests, followed by selection of specific courses.

In designing programs to fit their needs, it is necessary for students to take several achievement tests. Parents, student and advisor review student test results to identify strengths and weaknesses which, necessarily, will play a part in assessing what the pupil's school program will be. Plans and programs can, of course, be altered when necessary.

The advisor monitors the student's progress, with the guidance department help if needed, as he or she moves through high school. When and if difficulties are encountered, appropriate adjustments are made in the student's program.

The Ferguson-Florissant School District depends on what is called an Instructional Management System (IMS) to electronically collect and report student achievement data to be used in individual program planning. IMS also provides attendance data, student performance in the classroom and in extra class activities.

In addition to the two hours a week advisors usually spend working with their respective students one-to-one, advisors also meet for fifteen minutes once a week with their groups of students. At this time advisor and students prepare for the week ahead.

I attended a typical advisory group meeting conducted by an assistant principal. The group, consisting of four or five students from each grade 9 through 12, seemed to know and like each other. Today the principal concentrated on the coming second semester and encouraged students to ask questions about possible shifts in their schedules. Then he introduced a student who had joined their group for the first time, told where the student had gone to school before and urged everyone to help the newcomer learn his way around McCluer North.

Advisors often find that the two hours a week planned for consulting with their students, plus the Monday morning weekly group meeting, do not provide adequate time for advisory work.

Many advisors, therefore, use their preparation period time — in the six-period day each teacher has one hour for preparation — and after school and evening hours for advisory work with students. One teacher told me that contacting parents by telephone was also helpful, especially when both parents could participate in the conference at the same time.

"When I first entered McCluer North in the 9th grade," a student told me, "my parents, advisor, and I had an hour-long conference. We mapped out a four-year selection of subjects that seemed right for me. I seemed to be on track so we haven't needed three-way conferences very often. We have met at least once a year, and there are phone calls whenever they seem necessary. I think it's great to have someone at school to whom you can go whenever you want to."

One day I volunteered to take the place of an advisor who could not meet with his group at the usual time. I asked the students to write answers to two questions: "What do you think makes this school outstanding?" and "Who do you think is primarily responsible for its becoming outstanding?"

Of 35 responses, 20 dealt with the faculty ("a great faculty," "a creative faculty," etc.); 9 with the program ("diverse course offerings," "good sports program," "a good place to learn.") Others listed "clean, modern school site," "wide selection of activities and field trips," "good friends," and "parents are closely involved with teachers." None of them challenged the statement that their school was outstanding. They agreed "that the fact is established and we're proud of it."

When I asked them how they would improve the school if they had the opportunity, the majority said that the more deserving students should have more freedom. Other "should be's" included "increased trust of students," "better response to student complaints," "more pep assemblies," and "less waste of time in detention room."

While visiting McCluer North, the assistant principal in charge of scheduling, grade reporting, security and building needs, helped me in getting to know the school. But I noticed that every time I wanted to see him there were either students or a teacher talking with him. I asked him the reasons for so many conversations.

"The advisor is our major and basic contact between pupils and parents," he said. "The advisor's records, the records of the counselors, and our records here in the school office must mesh. Often students and I, and at other times teachers and I, discuss the same subjects, so it is important that we keep one another informed — that we all understand one another. This keeps the advisory system alive, alert and relevant."

4.

To give the school direction, McCluer North leans heavily on its Program Improvement Committee (PIC) which is made up of all department chairpersons, administrators, a guidance department representative and several designated teachers.

PIC's function is to check how the school is doing in its efforts to reach yearly goals. How well goals were attained one year are measured and adjustments are made as needed for the forthcoming school year.

PIC meets at least once a month but usually every week. The agenda usually deals with not more than two major items but more if needed. The greater part of a meeting I attended was spent discussing possible options for students who are unable to earn required credits.

An advisor, who was also the math department chairperson, raised the question: "What should we do about students who are not able to earn the two credits needed in mathematics to graduate?" Although one of his students was a hard worker and mixed well with others, he added, the boy was unable to retain sixth grade level math fundamentals. Nonetheless, the advisor did not think it would be in the boy's best interest to place him in a special education class, and he was confident that the student would make good in life if he found a job where positive personal qualities were more beneficial than math. He acknowledged that although the boy could be issued a certificate of attendance — something that had been done before for others — the problem deserved a better solution than that.

Some PIC members felt that such a pupil — one who, in spite of certain academic limitations — is judged capable of functioning as an adult in society — should be certified as completing high school if he has done his level best.

Perhaps, a member suggested, McCluer North should consider a third high school certificate to accommodate such students? Some time later I learned that this matter was resolved by developing highly specialized math courses to meet the needs of low achievers.

This example of how PIC operates to help McCluer North serve the needs of each student is only one of a long list of the committee's accomplishments.

5.

Department heads at McCluer North bear little resemblance to department heads in traditional schools of years past where one of their major considerations was to make sure there were enough textbooks for everyone. Today, at McCluer North, department heads are deeply involved in enriching the curriculum and in providing leadership in the school's on-going search to broaden learning opportunities for all of its students.

I attended a communications department meeting that began with the head of the guidance staff announcing that he would be visiting each 9th grade communications class to explain available guidance services. The communications department head next described a new creative writing workshop to be held for pupils planning to publish a literary magazine, and discussion followed on the advisability of utilizing a representative of the Scholars-in-Residence program to help enrich advanced composition.

Next, members shared mutual concerns about test score results that were not as high in English as in science and math. Many spoke of the "tight rope" they walk by resisting outside pressures to make McCluer North's English program become more memory oriented — while at the same time not short-changing pupils who, after graduation, will have to meet admission standards of institutions that place heavy emphasis on test results.

I talked with a department head about leadership at McCluer North. "We do not have a directive kind of leadership," she said. "Rather, our leaders select professional people who create the kind of environment that stimulates innovation. Department heads study chronically failing students to find out why they fail and what can be done about it. We look at test scores for college entrance. We look at whether students are meeting, or will be able to meet, requirements. We don't hesitate to change our methods or direction as needed. Our curriculum is not static. And every department regularly re-evaluates its own curriculum — another factor, I think, that makes our school outstanding."

From other department heads I learned of their concern about the growing popularity of the idea that schools should more vigorously pursue for their students what is commonly referred to as a more 'practical' education.

Some departments heads regard the suggestion as nothing more than a demand that schools 'train' rather than 'educate' their students. "We know from what we read, from the book Future Shock on down," a department head commented, "that jobs will not remain the same, that people will have to be educated in the humanities, in flexibility, in thinking logically, because things will rapidly become obsolescent and new roles will constantly evolve for our people."

6.

Teacher evaluation at McCluer North never stands still. School administrators begin by evaluating teachers on the job, determining which are fit or unfit to continue in the classrooms and which need help in improving skills. Then the school provides every opportunity for teachers to improve, to grow on the job, and to develop professionally to their utmost capabilities.

Each of the three assistant principals and the principal evaluates a fourth of the faculty each year. Department heads, too, are involved in evaluating the teachers working under their leadership. The process is thorough and requires considerable thought and time.

The principal and his assistants scrutinize three separate areas in their evaluation of classroom teachers: teacher goals, what is called an "Obvservation Cycle" study, and performance.

The goal review summary is completed by the teacher and used as the basis for the supervisor's observation and for conferring with teachers. The "Observation Cycle" study contains lesson objectives, observed teacher-student behaviors, description of the observation, and teacher comments.

The performance review lists criteria for determining effective teaching under the categories Classroom Management, the Teaching Act, Interpersonal Relations and the Professional Self. Performance levels are checked as outstanding, successful or unsuccessful, and space is provided for other comments.

When I asked principal Bill Hampton for his estimate on how many teachers he felt were really good in his school, he answered, "About three-fourths of our teachers are excellent in every respect. The rest are good on at least one part of their assignment but not overall." He added that during his sixteen years at McCluer North only four tenured teachers have been dismissed because of ineffectiveness and several probationary teachers were not rehired.

7.

Because modern educators realize that the strength of a faculty and of individual teachers depends as much on what is learned on the job as on what was learned in college and university, helping teachers to develop professionally, sometimes referred to as "in-service" education, is taken very seriously at McCluer North.

Staff development there occurs in many ways and takes many forms — from brief conferences between teachers in school lounges and halls to formal courses at colleges and universities.

As I walked through the halls and offices, I frequently observed chatting staff members. Two large, atttractively decorated and furnished staff conference rooms created an inviting atmosphere for teachers to share ideas and experiences. One room is used primarily for social studies and communications, the other for math and science — the four subject areas with the greatest number of teachers. Teachers in other departments frequently meet in smaller departmental offices.

In addition to these kinds of exchanges, teachers guide and sponsor a multitude of extra-class activities — all of which enhance their professional talents while enriching the education of students. But there are still other opportunities at McCluer North for professional growth.

McCluer North receives numerous invitations from other schools to tell about its advisory program. Generally, the principal is invited to speak, but he frequently suggests the name of one of the teachers to take his place.

One teacher told me of his trip to Oregon to speak to a high school staff about the advisory system. He said the experience increased his feeling of importance as a professional and taught him a lot about what the other school system was doing.

Competitions attract the interest and time of McCluer North teachers. A science teacher applied for a NASA astronaut assignment and was selected one of ten teachers to meet as a finalist in Washington, D. C. A social studies teacher was a finalist in the Missouri "Teacher-of-the-Year" competition, indicating the esteem in which he was held by his peers. Another social studies teacher was honored as Missouri's "Secondary Teacher-of-the-Year." In each instance, staff members helped their colleagues receive these types of recognition, and in so doing, undoubtedly became more sensitive to areas in which they themselves might improve.

Principal Bill Hampton does not exclude himself from in-service education. He has regularly attended summer seminars for administrators and was instrumental in founding and assuming an active role in a principals' academy for metropolitan St. Louis principals.

The Ferguson-Florissant School District is committed to the concept of staff development as a necessary adjunct to school improvement, a policy that has been of great value to McCluer North.

Besides initiating and directing programs for schools within its jurisdiction, the district also adheres to a liberal released-time policy for staff members who have the support of each school's leadership to take time off from their classes for worthwhile self-improvement projects. During the month of October 1985, for example, McCluer North teachers were granted fifty days of released time for staff development. Teachers used the time to attend conferences, workshops, seminars and institutes of state and national agencies.

The district also provides five orientation days in late August, five work days during the year, and two at the end of the year for teachers to plan, attend conferences and prepare for working with students.

8.

A positive, active relationship exists between students, parents and teachers at McCluer North. One parent described her experience during the enrollment of her son. "We were greeted so warmly," she remembered, "that he was immediately ready to start in his new surroundings. Even before we went to the school, several mothers had told me, 'Just wait and see how wonderful this is.' And they were right."

Another parent described her surprise, and pleasure, when she received a phone call one night from her daughter's advisor. "I couldn't believe that an advisor would take the initiative to call. Some of my friends told me that in their districts the parent always had to make the initial contact."

Appreciation for the school's math program was expressed by a third parent. Her son had taken algebra the year before and not liked it. He enrolled in geometry the next year and didn't like that either. His advisor called the boy's home one evening to discuss the situation with his parents. After analyzing the student's program and future goals with his math teacher, the advisor said, they both felt he might be better off taking consumer math instead of geometry. They had also consulted with his counselor, she was told, because he had more detailed records to check the soundness of their suggestion. The parents were very pleased. "We liked the recommmendation, our son liked it, and he is now happy in his new math class."

Other parents also commended the school staff for seeing to it that "youngsters who can't do advanced work have the opportunity to develop skills that will help them to get jobs, to be good citizens, to be proud of themselves."

Parents generally approved of the school's discipline policies and were grateful "the teachers follow up with the kids," although a few students told me their parents thought the teachers were sometimes too strict.

Although teachers and administrators are convinced that parents share an influential role in the schooling of their children, they also know that opportunities to meet with parents do not come easily, for family life today spins around a hectic job-related schedule. Nonetheless, avenues are found through which the staff can communicate face to face with parents, such as the open house held each fall, monthly advisory council meetings to which parents are invited, coffees sponsored by the assistant principals and parent advisory committee meetings sponsored by the principal.

Many activities at McCluer North are supported by interested parent groups. The athletic parent group numbers in the hundreds, as does the group supporting the band. Parents are also strong backers of drama and foreign language activities.

McCluer North had not had a PTA in its first 15 years. When asked why, Mr. Hampton said that in his experience he found PTA had often been so busy with "reading of the minutes" and other formalized procedures that its intended purpose — to get the school and parents to work together — never got off the ground. However, a strong feeling persisted in the school that the formation of a PTA would facilitate the exchange of ideas and concerns of parents and teachers, and a PTA was started in the school year 1987-1988.

Specialists from the community often become active partners with teachers at McLuer North and contribute much to the enrichment of classroom work. Especially effective are volunteers who discuss with students career choices and what qualities are needed to succeed on a job. I visited a class in which students were trying to understand more about child abuse and what could be done to lessen this condition in American homes. Knowing that bringing in people from the "outside" to present their views and share expertise has a profound effect on teen-agers, the teacher had invited a member of the police force to meet with the class. As a specialist in the field of child abuse, the officer's oral and slide presentations gave the young people a lot to think about.

In turn, community groups use the physical facilities at McCluer North. Community evening school, for example, utilizes McCluer North where about 280 individuals come each week for their adult education. By making reservations, civic and cultural organizations also utilize the building.

Rotary, Kiwanis, Lions and other clubs find the school eager to provide noon luncheon programs by sending individual students to speak or a group of students who have planned something special, either to entertain or inform.

Two school subject offerings make use of the community as laboratories. The first is known as the Community Outreach Program, which serves students who are interested in teaching or a related career. The students spend Monday through Thursday out in the community for about half a day, and then meet on Friday on campus with their teacher to summarize their experiences. When I talked with twelve of the pupils enrolled for the 1985-1986 fall semester in the Community Outreach Program, half of them said that they were going to continue the course for the next semester.

Some of the Community Outreach students were active at a school for the mentally retarded; others at elementary schools working with first graders or preschoolers. The majority of participants said they benefited from the program, adding that they enjoyed most working with children. This program helps students make career decisions, or perhaps equally important — decide what careers are not for them.

Second of the programs, the Community Learning Program (CLP — also a career exploration offering, but with a different slant) has been in the curriculum for 14 years. Students enroll in CLP for one semester of the school year with three classes a day, five days a week. Four days a week they leave the school for three periods to work under the supervision of a community sponsor who is active in the metropolitan area's business community. They meet back at the school Fridays with their teacher.

During 1981-1982, 140 questionnaires were sent out to McCluer North graduates to determine how they now felt about the work they had done in CLP while in high school. All who answered responded that CLP was "valuable," while most agreed that "it was the most rewarding experience" they had had in high school. Nearly all students said that CLP helped them to plan their goals, and in some cases to achieve them. And they added that CLP taught them more about themselves — to understand their own strengths and weaknesses.

Discussing CLP with students, I learned that their assignments covered a variety of enterprises. Four students had assignments in schools, three in hospitals, two at radio stations, one in the fire department and one in a retail electric appliance store. Their comments reveal some of the reasons for the popularity of this program:

> "I like the people I work with. I am interested in the patients and their illnesses. I like to see the doctors and nurses at work."
>
> "I like the atmosphere of the radio station. I can relate to the people there, and I especially enjoy learning all I can about sound equipment."
>
> "What I am doing here at school is to help students develop and maintain a better self-image. They seem to like to learn from someone their own age."

9.

It is bewildering to think of all the communities of which McCluer North is a part. There is, of course, the Florissant community itself, and the Ferguson-Florissant School District. There is also the St. Louis County and metropolitan St. Louis. There is the State of Missouri, and, finally, the United States.

Adjacent to McCluer North's campus is the city of Florissant's Civic Center which includes a swimming pool and auditorium. Rather than duplicating these facilities, an agreement between the city and the school permits students to use the civic center for both swimming and drama.

A cooperative district board, a strong district administration and help emanating from members of the district's central office, are responsible, in great part, for McCluer North's success. An annual high point in the district is its "Celebration of Excellence," event which gives recognition to the work of outstanding teachers.

Another reason attributed to McCluer North's excellence has to be that area citizens take seriously their responsibilities to elect outstanding system-wide administrators and staff members. They recognize the importance of electing a quality board of education — one that will employ outstanding system-wide administrators and staff members. They know that some board members might be more interested in representing special interest groups than in the education of young pupils, and that some system-wide administrators may be more interested in their own promotion to better jobs than in the development of good schools. So they do their best to elect the best.

McCluer North's faculty believes in a "bubble-up" rather than a "drip-down" school system — that is, leadership and initiative for change emerge best from teachers and a single school rather than only from top administrative structures. The principal and staff share a common philosophy: that good education demands a strong faculty.

A strong faculty, they agree, will make use of the best teaching programs that are available without surrendering authority to make final decisions — unlike some school "bookkeepers" who administer programs because they originated in the central office or from giant national companies selling learning materials.

Over the years, one of McCluer North's strengths has come from what is called the St. Louis cooperative superintendents' group. Originally organized with only superintendents in mind, the group has expanded to include board members and sub-groups representing elementary and secondary administrators as well as subject field staff members. The cooperative group helped to develop a special district for handicapped pupils and for vocational education. From this group also came initiatives to set up an audio visual department, now serving all of the county's school districts, and a community college district serving both the city of St. Louis and St. Louis County.

Missouri, like all other states in the union, elects governors and legislators who may or may not believe in strengthening public education. And many schools have learned that state departments of education can affect local school districts and individual schools either by their leadership or lack of it. Luckily for McCluer North, the state of Missouri's concerns for better schools have consistently produced both hope and support. Hope comes from the knowledge that in 1984 the State Board of Education adopted an action plan reaching for school excellence. Further, the Missouri General Assembly passed a law requiring the state department to identify key skills in English, social studies, mathematics, science, language arts, civics and reading, aimed at reflecting what students should know at the end of selected grade levels.

The impact of state legislation on the nation's individual schools was subsequently examined by the Association for Supervision and Curriculum Development (ASCD), a leading national education association: "No one questions the need for secondary school improvement," ASCD reported in the Los Angeles Times (1985), "but whether real and long-lasting improvement can result from the flood of mandates handed down from state legislatures is questioned," adding that "the states have thrown the balance in the high school curriculum 'out of kilter' by forcing all students to take more courses in conventional academic subjects and computer literacy. Vocational and fine arts courses and other electives are being squeezed in favor of more math and science."

McCluer North interacts with schools throughout the country in a variety of ways. Its membership in the North Central Accrediting Association is a plus, according to the school's principal who also added that the association is no longer feared as it was years ago but, rather, welcomed as a positive influence.

In addition, although McCluer North was the only public high school in Missouri cited in 1984-1985 for excellence by the U. S. Department of Education, information about its programs was disseminated to other schools throughout the nation by regional educational laboratories — illustrating how one school's success can help other schools improve.

Staff members also visit out-of-state schools to help them organize better guidance programs, while visitors are welcomed at McCluer North to observe the advisory program in action.

Maintaining control of its educational program, while at the same time cooperating with the many groups that are directly or indirectly related to the school, is one of McCluer North's finest achievements.

10.

Because McCluer North establishes a suitable learning climate, by its example of hard work and good relations in working together, most students feel good about the school and their teachers. These are some of the things I heard them say:

"You can see class principals anytime. They are always around. They listen."

"Teachers go to extra activities before and after school. They're interested."

"Teachers are willing to help you even if it means they have to spend time before or after school."

"Teachers support the academic clubs as well as sports."

"I haven't had a bad teacher yet and I'm a senior!"

At the time McCluer North received national recognition for excellence, *Polaris*, the school yearbook, conducted an essay contest. Students were to write what they thought their school did that made it worthy of receiving the award. Winning essays were assembled into a booklet named *In the Starlight*. Excerpts from several entries reveal some of the things that set this school apart from others:

First Student

"McCluer North students are treated and looked upon with a mature and respectful attitude. Students are given responsibilities that other schools wouldn't dream of giving their students. Students are allowed, when necessary, to be in the halls without identification cards; they are allowed to drive to school; they are allowed to walk the halls freely. Students are supplied with an open-spaced library where they can come and go without having to check in at the front desk. Treated with this kind of respect, most students do not want to attend school anywhere else . . . . Exchange students from Mexico, France, and elsewhere are welcomed with open arms. So if you are looking for a model to see how well an integrated school can work, take a good look at McCluer North . . . .

"At McCluer North, new and better teaching techniques have been adapted in all classes. Intermediate and advanced English courses use open discussions as well as lectures as part of the teaching strategies . . . . The subject of science may start with the development of life on earth and end with the study of the stars . . . . McCluer North offers general, intermediate and advanced honor classes. With these different levels, students are able to challenge themselves at their level of difficulty."

"McCluer North has outstanding teachers, offers an immense variety of classes, and encourages an informal setting in the school . . . Our advisory system is unique . . . Teachers use creative methods to get information across to the students by performing experiments, showing movies or videos, sponsoring field trips, using various audio visual equipment and having guest speakers . . . The enthusiasm the faculty show for their profession, their subject, and their students adds an extra spark to their teaching . . ."

Third Student

"Some people say that the diversified student body of a public school invites mediocrity. This is not so at McCluer North . . . The atmosphere of the school is relaxed and open, does not inhibit or restrict teachers or students . . . .The school offers a very liberal education; there are extremely challenging, thought-provoking classes for the highly motivated students and also more basic classes for those who need or want them. The word 'want' is important here because it exemplifies the fact that the administration has enough faith in high school students to allow them to design their own education within reason . . ."

"Everything in the system focuses on treating the students as rational, mature beings. Although McCluer North provides an intellectual, physical, and moral education, this is not done by telling students what to think. It is merely a stepping stone where students learn how to think and how to approach life . . . Students are taught to reach for the unreachable, and to never stop striving to make this world a better place to live in.' '

11.

One of the most unique aspects of McCluer North is its extensive offering of dynamic extracurricular activities — sometimes referred to as extraclass activities, club activities or simply activities. In 1983-1984, sixty to seventy activities occupied eighty percent of the students!

At McCluer North a club can be started by any student who finds a faculty sponsor willing to work with the group. After an initial announcement, and if enough students show up at the first meeting, a new club is born. Certain regulations govern club organization: Participating students must secure from teacher-sponsors passes to ride school buses which run every hour from the close of school until 6:00 p.m. to transport those taking part in after-school activities. In addition, any fund raising must be approved by the director of student activities.

Most of the clubs are organized for fun, for enjoying activities with friends. But they indirectly inculcate students with the feeling that McCluer North belongs to them — the school is their community for studying and learning. I asked several students how many clubs they belonged to and they answered from "three to ten" with six being the median.

A bulletin issued at the beginning of the year, prepared by the directors of student activities, lists available student activities: twenty-two clubs, ten student committees, eight performing groups, three publications, a marching band, a pompom corps, twelve girls' athletic teams and ten different sports for boys; cross-country, football with six coaches for several teams; three soccer programs, three basketball, three wrestling, two baseball, swimming, track, tennis and golf.

Activities vary from traditional groups such as chess, to new clubs such as "Dungeons" and "Odyssey of the Mind." Others develop as offshoots of the changing world in which we live — i.e., SADD (Students Against Drunk Driving).

Three different directors coordinate three different divisions of student activities: club and related regular school activities; athletics and related groups (band, cheerleaders and pompom); and academics.

Academics did not become a separate division until 1983-1984 with the appointment of a separate director. The director of academic activities regularly issues bulletins to bring the staff up to date on what is happening that may be of interest to them or their students. The February 1985 Academicians' Calendar, for example, contains the following information:

Essay contest of the Missouri Public Health Association. Scholarship award: $500

Missouri State Historical Society award of $300 for the best article on Missouri history

Names of team members competing in the U. S. Academic Decathalon

Names of six students who will represent McCluer North at the fifth annual TEAMS (Test of Engineering Aptitude, Mathematics and Science)

Poetry contest for students sponsored by Washington University. Prize: $1,000

Name of the student selected to represent McCluer North in the Missouri Regional Junior Science, Engineering, and Humanities Symposium

Details about the Mark Twain Festival: "Mark Twain, the Man, the Myth, and the Magic"

The director of academics helps teachers keep abreast of contests and available resources to supplement and motivate the work in their classes, including such items as: Ralston Purina Co. sponsors a symposium . . . A camera company sponsors a photography contest . . . Several other organizations have essay contests, one offering $2,000 as first prize.

As expected, athletic activities draw the greatest number of student participants. But nearly as many vie for band, cheerleading, and pompom as for sports teams.

Forty-eight girls recently made up one year's pompom group. One student, now in her fourth year as a pompom girl, had won an award in a metropolitan competition. I wanted to know what there was about this activity that she liked. Smiling, she said, "It's just like performing on the stage. It's fun working with the other girls. The only hard part is that there are five practice periods a week during the season — two of them at night."

Despite a rigorous sports program, athletes don't get too far removed from their studies. In a recent year, thirty senior varsity lettermen had a grade point average of 3.33 or higher: 4.0 is an A.

Because teenagers learn best at school when they feel free to express themselves, the school newspaper is one of the best places to look for signs of a healthy climate in which students can put this freedom of expression to work. *Stargazer*, McCluer North's student newspaper, has received many awards for excellence. Students write and publish articles in this publication not only to inform other students but parents and the entire community as well.

As I read back issues of *Stargazer*, I was impressed with the serious concern of the school journalists and their responsible treatment of school life issues. Integration of Kinloch High School students into McCluer North, for instance, received front page coverage in *Stargazer* on three different occasions — before desegregation occurred, at the time of the merger and after the students had been at McCluer North for a year. Excerpts from an article appearing in *Stargazer* (March 21, 1975) under the headline, "Integration Plan Readied," tells us a great deal about the young people at McCluer North as they move from adolescence to adulthood:

"This proposed integration plan involves a number of procedures for building a trust between students, parents, teachers, and administrators. Both McCluer North and Kinloch students have developed certain fears about each other which Principal Hampton hopes will be dispelled by the right kind of planning and activities."

A student is quoted in the "Merger Comes Off Smoothly" story of June 2, 1977: "The merger went through smoothly because students just accepted it and helped to dispel the rumors that were flying thick at the time . . . .Not only did students try to achieve a smooth transition, but the teachers also played a major role."

A year later a young journalist writes in the article "Merger Seems Successful" (October 8, 1986) of still another development: "There was much concern last year that McCluer North would change drastically due to the annexation of Kinloch. The merging of the two schools was awaited with a mixture of apprehension on the one side and hopeful participation on the other . . . .The combined efforts of both communities, Florissant and Kinloch, made possible an easier joining of the two schools. The faculty, the mayor, the students, parents and principals worked together to make it happen. Their purpose was also to insure that the unique qualities of both schools were kept."

An editorial in *Stargazer*, "Cover the Smokers," took the stand that while it was generally agreed that smoking isn't such a hot idea, smokers,

101

nonetheless, shouldn't be punished by being forced to light up in the school's only designated area — outdoors, on a barren piece of asphalt except for two benches and without any kind of protection from the weather. Perhaps, the editorial suggested, the school should seriously consider building an overhead shelter?

A second editorial, "Ruining School: No Pride At All," pushed hard against vandalism, and was especially severe against such petty acts as writing on lockers and carving on desks. "One would expect behavior like this from grade schools, but not high schools. Let's get with it . . . .A little concern among the students can go a long way. Let's keep our school free from the immature practices that deface McCluer North . . . "

"Odyssey of the Mind," part of a national trend to challenge high school students in their thinking, attracts a number of McCluer students. Under sponsorship of three staff members, "Odyssey of the Mind" members travel around the country where they compete with the keenest young intellects from other schools in solving thinking and reasoning problems. Judging from the discussions I heard, McCluer North students are very interested in this activity.

Recent competition involved creative problems dealing with "Technocrats," "Great Art Lives," and "Bridging the Gap." During the competition, "Technocrats" were required to design, develop and mass produce a product. "Great Art Lives" contestants selected two works from a list of great masters and were asked to paint or sculpt replicas of each of them. In the "Bridging the Gap" competition, students designed and built two structures made of 1 x 8 x 1 x 8 inch strips of balsa wood and glue, which had to conform to complex specifications.

Drama is also a popular activity at McCluer North where three full-length plays are produced each year. Every other year students direct and perform in nine one-act plays.

The foreign language department carries on an extensive scholarship and school exchange program. Thirty-five to forty students travel to foreign countries, in many instances exchanging places with students who come to McCluer North.

Each summer a scholarship fund established by the school's Interact Club (connected to the local Rotary Club) underwrites a student's trip to New Zealand where the visitor is provided room and board by a local family. In November, the process is reversed.

A second scholarship program, open to advanced students with three years of Spanish, provides a full academic year in Mexico. Again, Interact Club covers travel expenses (Rotary contributes a small stipend), and a Mexican family supplies room and board.

Still another scholarship program involves a three months' exchange with a West German student. In this instance the student contributes $600 to the program and supplies personal spending money. Remaining expense is paid by the Interact Fund.

102

Shorter exchange programs for advanced students are also part of foreign language department activities. A three-week, school-to-school exchange program includes exchanges with four schools: two French, one West German and one Mexican.

Surprisingly, general tax revenues underwrite only $6,000 of the school's cost of its extensive, far-reaching activities program. Publication of the school newspaper takes up half of that. Where does the rest of the money come from?

Ninety percent comes from customary miscellaneous money-making projects such as food and merchandise sales, as well as contributions. The foreign exchange program's Interact Club raises between $9,000 and $10,000 each year through its foreign festival and student talent show; a portion of the cost of the weight-lifting equipment ($2,800) was raised by the school; one of the clubs raised money for an autistic children's program.

The activity program sometimes develops problems that demand the attention of the faculty and the administration. With so much fund-raising going on, every effort is made to avoid taking on more projects than can be justified, to control or supervise efficient handling and accounting of funds. Some clubs suffer due to inadequate facilities. And when, for some reason, a staff member has to give up sponsoring a group, it is often difficult to find an appropriate replacement to fill the vacancy.

12.

The student council is an essential, but by no means the only, channel for student participation in school government. It provides boys and girls with lessons in weighing issues, making plans and carrying them into action. Student activities operate largely on their own, but the student council tries to help when problems arise because of duplication of effort or where special needs arise.

I attended a council meeting to see at close hand how it operated. About fifty students were present. One item on the agenda was the introduction of candidates for second semester officers. Each candidate spoke briefly so members would get to know the candidate's background and ideas. Another item on the agenda was a discussion about whether the council should collect food for needy families or contribute to the Statue of Liberty Fund. After that, the group decided to undertake the food collection project and proceeded to plan how it would be done.

I talked with the president of the student council, a senior, who had presided at the meeting. He was articulate about the council's role in student government, enumerating the alternatives or routes McCluer North students could pursue to make it a good school. He was not particularly perturbed that the council was not the coordinator for all student government activities. In our talk, I learned that this young man was also president of

SADD (Students Againsts Drunk Driving), an organization he was convinced was very useful at the school.

13.

We now come to an intruiging piece of evidence of student participation in school governance. When the Ferguson-Florissant district was enlarged with the addition of Kinloch and Berkeley districts, the judge also mandated creation of a Student Relations Committee which would consist of an equal number of black and white students. Its function was, and is, to create better understanding between the races. Members of this group are called upon for help if difficult situations arise. They meet weekly and have as their sponsors two faculty members.

I attended an after-school meeting of SRC which had been called to plan events for a Brotherhood Week. Programs considered were an assembly, a brotherhood breakfast, a progressive dinner or a brotherhood ball. The faculty sponsors entered into the discussion only slightly during the first hour of the meeting. Students felt completely at ease in expressing themselves, offering their ideas, not trying to say what the sponsors might want them to say. After a long discussion, a faculty sponsor highlighted some points that he thought students would have to face to have a good Brotherhood Week in less than a month's time. The group agreed that one meeting would not do it; more meetings were needed if good planning were to occur.

I spoke with a student member on the Student Relations Committee. "First semester we had group seminars which consisted of over seventy students at each session," he told me. "We wanted to get student opinions on the benefits and solutions of being part of the 1976 desegregation plan, also known as the merger."

"Second semester we went into the classrooms and asked students to complete a questionnaire that had been prepared by SRC. By the close of the school year, we had interviewed over half of the student body on race relations and how to improve them and received excellent responses. Overall, SRC considers itself successful."

While visiting a group of black girls at the SRC meeting, I learned about the Young Ladies of Elegance. These young ladies, with the sponsorship of a former Kinloch teacher, carry on the tradition of having a ball — a "coming-out" party. They take it very seriously and it seems to be a positive influence in their lives.

One member addressed a group on the benefits of belonging to the club. "I have been a member of Young Ladies of Elegance for about a year. I like being a part of it is because it gives me an opportunity to learn the behaviors of a young lady. Another reason is that it helps to develop the real person inside of you so you can accomplish your future goals. And it gives you an opportunity to help people in need. When you have done a good job at this, you are proud of yourself."

104

14

There is good student discipline at McCluer North. Here, again, the advisement program's influence is felt and is generally credited with the success of maintaining harmony and order among students. A special relationship develops between student and advisor, a direct result of private conferences or group advisory meetings. Parents get progress reports four times a year. Personal contacts with teachers are not reserved for "trouble," but to celebrate student successes as well.

People at McCluer North refer to their advisory system as a "family approach" to school management. Along with the friendly family approach, there is the faculty conviction that teachers must lead students to projects and learnings in which students will take an interest. Once this is done, disciplinary problems all but disappear.

"I recall the case of a girl who, during the first part of the semester, was a real discipline problem," Principal Hampton relates. "No one could find a clue to what would make her productive. Then she got involved in doing a sculpture for her art class, and it won first prize in our spring show. Now she's involved in plans to build the same sculpture but on a much larger scale, big enough to be a piece of playground equipment. It will be perfect for that. It has planes for sliding down and corners for hiding in. The change in that girl after involvement in her art project has been a joy to see . . . ."

Penalties are consistent, firm, and fairly administered. The student handbook spells out rules and regulations regarding student discipline. Topics covered include dress code, attendance, absence, late arrivals, tardy policy, leaving campus and drug abuse. The handbook stresses that radios and tape players, card playing, gambling and playing games not directly related to instruction or an extracurricular activity, are not permitted on campus.

There is a mutual understanding between staff and students: Students who don't comply with reasonable standards should not "get by" with their misbehavior. Rules are explicit: A student is tardy if he/she is not in the assigned seat when the tardy bell rings. Teachers will give one warning for unexcused tardies and will assign a detention for the second and subsequent tardies.

Grade level assistant principals handle minor infractions, and teachers get help in dealing with student misbehavior if and when they need it.

One teacher, supervising a detention room after school, estimates that, on an average, about twelve students arrive each afternoon.

Isolation from peers, or suspension, is recognized as a more serious disciplinary regulation than detention. During a school year, about eleven percent of the students are suspended, including in-school suspension as well as being sent home.

Transfer to an alternative school is also considered a disciplinary measure because it removes students from their friends. The alternative school's educational program is purposely less departmentalized, concentrating more on a "levels of accomplishment" approach, giving students more opportunity to succeed at their own pace.

Use of drugs and alcohol results in assignment for four weeks to a special classroom located within the district but not on school campus. Parent participation in this program, through family counseling, is mandatory.

Within the framework of the district's discipline policies and regulations, each spring McCluer North evaluates the effectiveness of its discipline program and examines all data on suspensions. Based on this analysis, new goals are set for the following year.

Convinced that positive student reinforcement is a major factor in warding off possible discipline problems, McCluer North recognizes and rewards good work. Students can strive for honors in nearly all subjects. To obtain these honors students must be enrolled in courses for credit beyond the high school graduation requirement and must earn a mark of 3.5 on a 4.0 scale. Recognitions are awarded at an honors assembly and recorded as permanent student records. At the 1984-1985 honors assembly 65 seniors were recognized for winning scholarships which totalled $71,000.

Besides monetary awards, recognition of work well done is communicated in other ways. The daily bulletin is usually filled with news about student awards; and bulletin board areas are loaded with student art work, awards and achievements.

15.

The only way to learn firsthand how students spend their time in classrooms is to go there — not to casually look around and leave — but to become part of their classes. That's what I did. The assistant principals responsible for coordinating grades 9, 10, 11, and 12 helped me pick four students that I could accompany during the day.

My first student was Julie S., a 9th grader who planned to be an airline attendant when she finished four years of high school. Her classes started with French, followed by Astronomy, Algebra, Health, English and Introduction to Social Studies.

As the French period opened, the teacher discovered that the projector for the film she planned to show had not yet arrived. While she took care of the problem, some students asked to take a test that they had missed and went to the small enclosures at the back of the room to do this. In a short time, the projector arrived and the film was shown. The teacher asked questions. Most were quickly answered. The teacher's manner was warm and her approach informal. On our way out, Julie told me that she likes her French class and plans to take it all four years. Maybe, she said, a knowledge of French will help her in securing a job with an airlines company.

As soon as the Astronomy (2nd hour) bell rang, the teacher reminded the students to continue work on the assignment started the day before: To calculate the rate of rotation of the sun by checking the movement of sunspots. He reviewed the steps to be taken: Measure the angles twice for each latitude, label the angles, make sure to put the work in orderly steps. No time was lost. Students went to the lab area to get rulers and compasses, immediately got out their worksheets and drawings, and started to work. Julie, a white girl, sat next to a black boy. They helped each other — which seemed to be the order of the day rather than each student working alone. The teacher moved swiftly around the room, aiding students when they asked for help.

Julie said the work was very hard for her in Astronomy, and that she was taking it to satisfy one of two required science years. She also thought it might help her if she decided to go into airline work since the subject dealt with space. She said she had asked to take Physical and Life Science which she thought was more in line with her interests, but her advisor told her that her grade point average was so high that she ought to take Astronomy. Next semester she would take Cell Biology.

Julie's 3rd hour was Algebra taught by a black teacher. (Her first two hours were taught by white teachers.) There had been a test the day before, and the teacher reviewed the exercises. Student interest was high, and some volunteered to demonstrate their correct solutions at the board. Others asked questions about their mistakes. The teacher was open and warm in his approach to students, and the students respected the rights of others by not interfering or disturbing.

In Julie's Health class, several movies were shown and she took notes to prepare for tests. Today's study unit was on smoking — the day before students had finished a unit on drugs. Julie mentioned that Health was required of everyone for one semester.

"I like English best," she said. "I like to write — to be creative, but I like Social Studies, too," she added. "We learn many different things. So far it's been primarily geography with a lot of emphasis on map study, but I'm also learning how to study at school and at home, how to take tests and what I can do to improve in all of my classes."

I asked freshman Julie how she thought she was going to like McCluer North during the next four years. "I'm sure I'm going to enjoy it," she said. "There are so many people to get to know and there are many things to do. Everybody gets involved."

I next accompanied Denita W., a sophomore. Her six classes were Physical Education, Biology, Health, Careers, English and Social Studies. (English and Social Studies are combined to make a core.)

The P. E. class, a cross-section of sophomore students, played soccer in the gymnasium on the day I visited with Denita, who was a goalie. You could not help but see how proud she was when she kept the other side from scoring. The class was divided into two groups so that each student played half a period. Everyone seemed to enjoy the spirited competition. I learned that all Physical Education classes begin with a calisthenics warmup. While I watched the soccer game from the bleachers, one of the girls nearby asked me why I was visiting. I told her I wanted to find out all I could about the program at McCluer North. "This is a great school," she volunteered. "Why?" I asked. "Because," she answered, "the students and the teachers make it good."

On the way to her next class, I asked Denita about her past schooling. She told me that until the past summer she had lived in St. Louis, but she didn't like the high school she attended there — there were too many fights. "But," she hastened to add, "not at McCluer North."

The day I visited Denita's Biology class, the topic for study was lungs and breathing, with emphasis on the rib cage and the action of the ribs and the diaphragm in breathing. After the teacher's presentation, there was a test. Students were encouraged to consult their books or refer to the lab manual in answering the questions. Each high school, I was told, decides on the biology books and learning materials it wishes to use. The teacher assigned homework, reminding students that their written work should be in complete sentences. On our way out, the teacher told me that the science department staff had agreed that current topics related to science should be part of the curriculum, and that AIDS was a subject each of them would soon have to address in their classes.

Denita and I went to her third period class, Health. As 9th grader Julie had previously told me, smoking was a prominent subject in health classes. The teacher led off by writing on the board detailed points about smoking — More Women than Men Smoke, Why People Continue to Smoke, Why Some People Have Decided to be Nonsmokers, "Cold-Turkey" — Stopping Abruptly, and Big Reasons Why Smoking Doesn't Pay Off — then turned on an overhead projector to show transparencies. The period included a mix of lecturing and pupil responses.

Moving on with Denita to her fourth class, Careers, we were told that a test would be given (true or false, multiple choice and matching questions) on labor relations, the unit studied during the two weeks earlier. To save class time and when it appeared that most students had finished their tests, the teacher read various job descriptions and pupils tried to identify them. Students who had not finished their exams were encouraged to do so before taking part in the job identification exercise.

I was not able to accompany Denita to her core classes that afternoon, but I did learn that English and Social Studies were combined into a two-hour block with the work adjusted to the ability level of the pupils in the class.

Bob C., an 11th grader planning to attend an academically centered university such as Stanford, was designated as my next student to shadow. Bob was an outstanding athlete at McCluer North — his latest achievement being the scoring of two touchdowns to win the football game the previous

Saturday. He was modest and interested in learning — a good example of a high school student able to balance athletics and scholarship.

The first class for Bob was Calculus. Today's Calculus subject: Cartesian coordinates. The teacher asked students which problems that had been assigned for homework gave them the most trouble. Although it took only a few minutes to fill the board with problems that concerned the students, the teacher had no difficulty in securing volunteers to solve each of them. The teacher's soft, positive, articulate approach showed respect for everyone and made the class a satisfying one to visit.

As we moved from first to second period classes, Bob told me that he had taken Algebra in the 8th grade, Geometry in the 9th grade, Advanced Algebra in the 10th. Now, in the 11th grade, he was taking Calculus but hadn't decided what to take in the 12th.

Bob's second hour was Anatomy, a subject he said he particularly liked and which might influence him in choosing his vocation. I sensed that Bob was already reasonably clear that his career would be related to math and science. While in Anatomy, I heard announcements from over the loudspeaking system, with Principal Bill Hampton congratulating groups of students who had made outstanding achievements the previous week. Students listened avidly and were obviously pleased when their names were mentioned.

The teacher said at the beginning of the period that there would be a diversion from their regular study in Anatomy in order to discuss a present day serious problem — AIDS.

I hadn't expected so soon to find a Science teacher doing what the Biology teacher had told me only the previous day was their practice — to interrupt the sequence of routinely scheduled subjects, when appropriate, to discuss current science-related topics. I still marvel when I recall my visit to that Anatomy class and the skill of the teacher. Her ability to discuss in a completely positive way the different aspects of the AIDS problem, which, until the 1980s was not generally talked about in our public schools, was a revelation. I have seldom seen such rapt concentration on the part of a high school class as I did during this presentation and discussion. The observer could only imagine what was going through the minds of students regarding the realities of being sexually active at the high school level, the ways that AIDS can be acquired, and the costs of this rapidly spreading disease to the individual and to society.

My shadow student's third class was Western Civilization. The teacher listed the sequence of units to be studied each quarter during the school year: Ancient Near East, Ancient Greece and Rome, Medieval and Early Modern Times and Modern History. Almost immediately, a student asked, "What is the meaning of Monotheistic God?" which brought on a spontaneous discussion of Hinduism, Christianity and Judaism.

The teacher next took questions from students concerning the long-term independent class projects they were to choose. From there, discussion moved to the subject of tribes and how they progressed from villages to states to nations, and then, sometimes to empires.

Bob and I spent our next hour in Chemistry where the message "Inch by inch — anything is a cinch," greeted us from the blackboard as we entered the room. The previous day's assignment, which included five equations in the lab manual, was reviewed by the teacher. Volunteering students put their solutions on the board, and the rest of the period was spent moving through their explanations. Students who had experienced no difficulty with the assignment were encouraged to move ahead into new work.

We began Bob's fifth class in the weightlifting room, an up-to-date, well equipped workout room with sound-absorbing carpeting over much of the floor. (I was told later that the cost of this room was $28,000, with the school providing $10,000 and the McCluer North student body raising the remaining $18.000.) Entering the room, Bob knew exactly what to do and wasted no time. He began with required warmup exercises designed to avoid injury and proceeded to specific weightlifting exercises prescribed for his physical development strategy.

During 6th period in Bob's British Literature class, we watched the film, "The England of Elizabeth." Discussion and questions following the film took most of the period, after which the instructor and class reviewed plans for the next day's work.

Senior Dwayne F., my last "shadow" companion, planned to attend Southeastern Missouri University. I got my signals crossed and missed visiting Dwayne during his first hour class. I thought he was to be in an advanced seminar, and I sat entranced in the class for nearly half a period listening to a discussion on John Stuart Mills' philosophy on liberty before I realized I was in the wrong place. Here, respecting their maturity, the teacher presented his material to the class in adult language. They listened intently, as the discussion evolved into a consideration of present day intolerance and whether war could ever be eliminated as a way to resolve conflict.

When I finally caught up with Dwayne, we had some free time to talk. He considered McCluer North's advisory system the school's most important single attribute, singling out counseling as a major help to students. Electronics studies and the "wonderful sequence of mathematics courses" were mentioned as school pluses. And, he added, he was appreciative that he could take honors courses in fields outside of his major interest. To my question "What do you think caused McCluer North to develop into such a good school?" he answered, "The staff works hard at making it a good school. Teachers are always asking students what they think."

Dwayne's second period, Advanced Chemistry, began with a short lecture by the instructor during which he used an overhead projector. Next, students went to the lab area and, in small groups, started their experiments, helping one another as they proceeded. Everything was orderly.

110

Students were absorbed in their tasks. The teacher circulated around the lab, ready to give a hand to any student or small cluster of students having difficulty.

Advanced Composition was Dwayne's third class. The teacher emphasized the need to plan intelligent use of long blocks of time. Review of the class schedule showed that note-taking would be the next unit to be explored and that it would last two weeks. Of special interest to students was the subject of how to study.

Dwayne's fourth period was spent as a "teacher's assistant" to the chairperson for Social Studies. He went to the teachers' lounge to find out how he could help, and was asked to take various records to the office and then to collect some items from other social studies teachers.

When seniors have a 3.75 grade point average (Dwayne qualified) they are permitted to be on their own, and during his fifth period, Dwayne elected to study Advanced Analytical Geometry.

Electronic Circuits occupied Dwayne's sixth hour class. Dwayne knew what he was supposed to do and went to his assigned drawer to get the necessary materials, allowing me time to talk with his instructor. If feasible, the instructor told me, the students are allowed to work with partners. He was relieved, he said, to see the national trend toward recognizing the importance of courses in electronics.

Electronic Circuits is the first course in the electronics sequence and is part of Dwayne's plan to concentrate in this field at the state university.

16.

Although I wasn't able to shadow the faculty in the same way I shadowed some students during my month-long visit at McCluer North, many staff members shared their thoughts with me about what they considered most productive or most worrisome in their teaching efforts. Here are selected reactions, views, and opinions:

"Improving students' reading skills and getting them to love reading is a No. 1 objective for many teachers at McCluer North. In my class, we read short, easy novels and short stories to improve students' reading ability. I read in class and then assign 10 pages of homework on which I quiz them the next day. Improving their writing skills is another goal.

"Once a week students do what we call 'free writing.' The next day, without revealing the authors' names, I read most of these papers aloud. Someone always asks if I am going to read his or her free writing today. I've seen spectacular improvement because kids were turned on by having an audience."

"I also give them dictation once a week so they can practice putting the periods and capitals in the right places. Another regular weekly activity is paragraphing. Each student must write a perfect paragraph. This gives me

111

a chance to tell each one that he or she has done well. The encouragement changes their attitudes about writing and helps them improve."

"We have read *Fahrenheit 451, Brave New World,* and *1984.* A good deal of time is spent on the issues raised by books, not on literature as such. The theme of the course is the "20th Century, Its Dangers and Promises." Students generally decide that nuclear arms, overpopulation, and environmental damage are the biggest dangers. I want them to realize that they need the facts on both sides of any issue before making a judgment. I want them to learn to value the environment of this planet and to participate in this democracy." - Communications Teacher

"I think we all work very hard here. There are so many roles to play, so many things expected of us and that we expect of each other. We work hard, and hard work produces good results.

"We have done some peer reviewing, on invitation, of each other's classes. We have a wide variety of styles in our department — very traditional, very laid back, very group oriented, very didactic. As long as teachers can produce well, their style is respected." – Communications teacher

"An educator must communicate a sincere willingness to help. An educator must be prepared, for without preparation there is disorganization and apathy. There must be direction to learning, for without goals students have nothing to strive for. There must be purpose for learning, for without purpose the experience is meaningless. There must be involvement, for without involvement there is alienation." – A Science teacher

"When low achieving students enter our core program, about 20 percent of them are ready to try hard. Eighty percent require a high degree of motivation. We strive to help them learn to read and write more effectively, starting with where they are, and to help them to develop better study skills.

"I like to call my method 'tough love.' Students can tell whether you care for them or not. When they realize that you do care for them, they will stay with you even when you have to be tough in your demands on them." - A Social Studies teacher

"As we move into the future, we must keep our curriculum strong for the highly motivated students, those who have high achievement and are college bound. We must emphasize and expand our offerings for the students who are not going to college but directly into jobs. And we have a financial problem, too. The world is moving ahead rapidly, and education, to keep its strength and to get stronger, must attract and keep highly talented teachers."

"We must keep the 3Rs front and center, but we can't stop there. We have to move on to help students learn to set and achieve goals in problem-solving and in thinking." – A Social Studies teacher

"As state and university requirements change and the student population changes, program changes will have to keep up to meet the needs of our students. We cannot give up our strong commitment to academic excellence just because fewer students may be going to the university in the future. We must avoid watering down our courses and at the same time develop new and challenging courses for those who are not headed for the university.'' – A Communications teacher

<h1 style="text-align:center">17.</h1>

As I sum up the facts and meaning of McCluer North, I am impressed first of all by the variety and richness of courses the school offers its students. Thirty different English courses appear in the 1985-1986 school catalog. In Foreign Language, every pupil progresses in terms of his or her individual growth in facility to use the language being studied.

I am impressed by the different approaches McCluer North uses for different types of students — the "average" student, if there is such a thing; the student of high ability; and the low-achieving student; or put another way, the student who needs extra help to succeed academically as well as socially and emotionally.

The alternative school, for example, serves students who need more personalized attention and who work better in a less complicated environment than exists at most McCluer North classrooms. Students who have difficulty earning credits in math in the regular classes are assigned to Basic Math or General Math; core English and American History are available for students with special academic needs.

Students who are unable to complete an entry level course in paragraph writing enroll in a writing lab. Tutoring in certain subjects can be arranged on request. For the student with extreme difficulties the special district program is available, with an Individual Education Plan (IEP) required to try to meet the needs of special education students.

I am impressed that the staff at McCluer North is as concerned about students who are having difficulty in learning as they are about students who are so outstanding that regular classes do not challenge them enough. Outstanding students are challenged through the school's college credit program, arranged with the metropolitan university. Extremely beneficial is advanced enrollment at a university, for students who can qualify, in a course beyond the usual starting work in that university.

The honors grade point system is noteworthy because it allows students to take advanced work in subject fields outside of their primary interest without running the risk of cutting down on their grade point average. Students can take Calculus, English and Social Studies seminars, Advanced Science courses and a 4th or 5th year of Language under this system.

I am impressed by the wide variety of "elective" courses. These permit students to follow their "elected" interests rather than being confined to taking only those courses that the school thinks are good for them.

I am impressed with the physically appealing openness of classrooms and the building as a whole. And the fact that activities are so often an outgrowth of classroom work helps students understand that McCluer North really has two faces: classroom mastery of academic subject work in addition to activities for recreation and cultural pursuits. The staff constantly strives to interweave music and the arts with its activity program, with life outside the school, and with the academic subjects such as English, Math, Science and Social Studies.

I am impressed that Artists-in-Residence projects play a big part in stimulating students' interest in the arts. For example, Bob Katz, an environmental sculptor and an art instructor at the University of Maine in Augusta, visited in 1984; and James Nicholson, a St. Louis playwright, came in 1985 to help students in playwriting and essay writing. Both artists worked at the school for a month. These projects were funded by the National Endowment for the Arts, Young Audiences, with help from the Missouri Arts Council, and the school district, when needed.

Students are not the only beneficiaries of such visits, however, for through observation, teachers also learn how to improve their work with students in the world of art.

The basic skills, to be learned well and retained, need to be practiced in meaningful settings, staff members told me, and reading and computation skills can be learned most effectively when students are motivated. That's where the advisors come in: Their job is to help students have a reason for going to high school.

I am impressed with the administrative philosophy that exists at McCluer North: Principal Bill Hampton and other school administrators are clear on the point that the best learning will occur if teachers feel they own their classrooms. He believes that sound planning provides the opportunity for the staff to arrive at common goals. He believes, too, that once this happens, teachers can do whatever they think is best to create an environment that is good for learning. Freedom to run one's own classroom, rather than fitting into a prescribed operating mold, means that different teaching styles are acceptable and are being practiced by different teachers.

Some teachers lean heavily on lectures or presentations. But more teachers have the knack for letting what they say turn into discussions, centered around questions asked by students. A few teachers believe in planning to the extent that they take time at the beginning of the semester to have students themselves set up specific goals for the course.

Then they figure out what activities should be carried on to try to reach those goals. Finally, they decide what kind of evaluation would be most effective to find out how well the group did in reaching the agreed-upon goals.

"When I visit a classroom," Bill Hampton says, "I look at the effect of the teaching on the students, how they are responding. I encourage teach-

114

ers to try different methods until they find those that work best. When I go into a classroom and feel good about what I see, I tell the teacher. I also go out and tell other people that what I saw was tremendous, and the word usually gets back to the teacher that I thought it was good.''

As teachers assume responsibility for what happens in their classrooms, they also believe that the school as a whole should have a degree of independence to work with students and parents. They fear the appointment of a future principal who will decide what teachers ''should do'' in their classrooms, and they fear inheriting a central office administration that would send out directives on what ''should happen'' in each classroom.

Talking with teachers at McCluer North and visiting their classrooms indicates that this is not a faculty that feels it has ''arrived'' just because it was recognized nationally as an outstanding school. Doing their present job the best they can, they also look to the future and have many concerns. Emphatically they agree that the advisory system must always be an integral part of the school.

The staff doesn't limit its vision to immediate problems. This faculty is looking into the 21st century and hopes it did a good job in getting the students of the 1980s ready for their adult roles. McCluer North's teachers have accepted the challenge to provide a school environment in which black and white students can learn to live and work together.

CHAPTER FIVE

Volunteers: Builders of Better Schools

School volunteers — those people who of their own freewill and without pay contribute time and energy — can make the difference between a school being ordinary or extraordinary. Although frequently visible in the school classrooms, workshops, libraries, gyms, playgrounds or cafeterias, they are also to be found in the community's banks, hospitals, restaurants, offices and industries.

In whatever form voluntary cooperation takes place, involved participants quickly discover that schools do not stand alone. Almost immediately they become aware of the partnership that exists between teachers and parents, between schools and communities, between districts and cities and finally between states and the federal government.

Odds are against a school being acclaimed "excellent," or even "good," if it does not consistently receive the active support of individuals or organizations outside the school. It is possible, of course, for schools to operate only with resources from within and many of them do, but if they are to fulfill their important role in the nation's development, they must be nourished by additional help from outside the school. Recognizing this importance, effective administrators and committed teachers work hard to cultivate a school climate that encourages community participation.

Bill Hampton, principal of McCluer North High School, admits that "If we hadn't gotten people interested and involved, we would have had a difficult time persuading the Board of Education that what we were doing made sense."

And Judy Endeman, Twin Peaks Middle School principal, concedes that because "we have the students for 6-1/2 hours a day and parents and the community have them for 17-1/2, what we are able to accomplish is multiplied only in relation to the degree of support we get from parents as volunteers."

Peggy Geren, Garden Hills principal, assessed this way the importance of outside support at the elementary school level: "The exchange that goes on between those of us both inside and outside the school stimulates us to tailor our programs to the individual child's needs."

Help is not limited to the contributions of parents concerned with a particular school because they may have children there; other citizens also donate considerable time to schools whose needs are made known. While involvement may initially begin within the school, it does not always end there, for volunteers frequently go on to fill important roles throughout the district, state and national levels.

A Garden Hills "freewiller" reminds us that "anyone who thinks seriously about volunteering must either enjoy working with or around children." If they don't, she emphasizes, their donation of time and energy will never produce the kinds of rewards or satisfactions mentioned by volunteers quoted in this study. It should not be undertaken by someone who inevitably ends up wishing they were some place else. It is important, therefore, that the right people become involved in the right place or job.

Most personal perhaps is the contribution of individuals who offer their services to work either one-on-one with students or with small groups in the classroom. "When you have 25 students in a high school's industrial arts class, the instructor can't demonstrate how to use heavy equipment — which can be dangerous and needs a minimum of distraction — and show someone how to read a ruler at the same time," a caring craftsman from the community explained, "so I help out by working side-by-side with any student who needs detailed help in learning how to cut or measure wood. If the teacher had to do it alone, he couldn't give more than an average of two minutes per student."

Because some students in the middle school woodshop finish their classroom work faster than others, they can turn to the teacher's "no-pay right-hand" who keeps them busy while the rest of the students catch up. He is proud of the role he had in helping students to design and build a lost-and-found rack which won a county fair ribbon. "It makes me feel good to know that I am doing something useful in a field I know something about."

A little bit of extra help in learning to read and in related subjects, such as literature and library research, goes a long way. At Garden Hills, a parent described her role in dealing with four boys who were consistently disruptive while the teacher tried to work with her reading group. The parent stressed the students' need for individual attention, someone who could stay close to them, to keep them engaged in their work, "so the students and I sat at another table in the room, removed from the others, where we could work together at our own pace."

Another parent worked with the school librarian, either at the checkout desk, cataloguing, taking inventory or performing other clerical jobs that

117

any library requires. "Without some volunteer help," she said, "the librarian would be hard pressed to get her job done."

Students reading below their grade level, and ESL (English as a Second Language) students in particular, seem to blossom from the input of volunteers. A citizen in the middle school district taped a number of books for the school's reading lab. In addition, one hour each week he led a discussion group of six 7th grade students, during which they exchanged views on topics of current interest.

Math lends itself well to the concept of individualized attention. A citizen who helped out at Twin Peaks described her work in a 7th grade math class: "I take two or three students who have a particular math problem and we go to the library to work on that problem. Separating such students from their peers, whom they often regard as being 'smarter' than they, helps them to relax and learn in a more comfortable setting."

Other tasks performed by teacher assistants include routine correcting of papers, entering grades into the records, adding up totals, and transferring information to report cards. A retired bookkeeper finds these jobs at Twin Peaks "right down my alley. I love it." Now in her fourth year of assistance, she is convinced that "the time I spend helping the teacher in any way I can gives her more quality time to spend with the students. She appreciates it and I appreciate it."

Students often get tired of seeing the same authority figures in school, day in and day out, so when someone from the "outside" comes in to offer personalized input, students instinctively sit taller and listen more attentively. This is especially noticeable when the guest(s) bring with them not only talk but articles and objects that can be seen, passed around and touched.

Such was the case when the Belkins, husband and wife in the Twin Peaks area, were invited to address the 7th grade social studies class studying the Middle East. The Belkins had recently returned from Israel, armed with a wealth of information, slides and artifacts. They passed around newspapers, money, bus tickets and handicrafts among the students. They answered questions. Mrs. Belkin recalls, "The fact that the newspapers were in a language unlike our own came as a surprise to the class! From the Israel museum, we brought back some beginning alphabets which showed how they were related to the Hebrew alphabet, reading right to left instead of left to right. The students couldn't believe it."

"I am convinced that merely reading about cultural differences," Mrs. Belkin continued, "does not make the same impression on young people as talking with someone who has been a part of it. After each session — we addressed two classes, each of which took two periods — there was much applause and all of the kids came up and thanked us."

The Twin Peaks Mystery Guest Program is ideally suited for community participation, for by the time students have quizzed the guest (following the format of TV's "What's My Line?"), they are eager to learn more about the "line" by asking more questions and getting more answers. When a local businesswoman appeared before 6th graders and discussed her vocational area, banking suddenly became a lively subject for learning.

Atlanta businessman Fred Vetter, president of Educational Solutions, and other Atlanta and national leaders, have provided Garden Hills Elementary School with a computer education classroom. Dr. Vetter is often at the school, conferring with teachers about the role of computer technology in education — he learning from them and they from him.

Junior Achievement, the nationally respected program in which business and industry cooperate with students to guide them through the process of developing a product, marketing it and earning a profit, is called Project Business at Twin Peaks. Officials of the firm of Hewlett-Packard have long been participants in Project Business, generally spending one period per week with a class. "We feel appreciated and think we are doing something worthwhile," a Hewlett-Packard representative said. "The students seem to get a lot out of it."

All learning does not, of course, take place in the classroom. What young people may labor over one week from a textbook becomes instantly clear when they visit a historic site or an operational example of something they are studying. But "field trips" take planning, supervision and responsibility, and teachers always appreciate the help of parents and other interested people who make these excursions easier to manage. One Twin Peaks parent, who had recently assisted on a trip to the nuclear power plant at San Onofre, described her trip. "We learned what happened in Chernoble, why it happened, and why the people at San Onofre think it cannot happen here."

Another Twin peaks parent talked of his involvement at the school with his son's Ski Club. "I served as a sponsor and drove one of the cars to the Mammoth ski area. Outings like these give parents and young people a chance to share a short vacation together. About half the students went by bus with parents and staff members who served as chaperones. The other half, with parents in charge, drove in automobiles."

One spring, eighteen parents, fifty children, and two 5th grade teachers from Garden Hills took a three-day trip which included the Okefenokee National Wildlife Refuge, the beach on the Georgia coast and Jekyll Island. One of the parents accompanying the children remembered that "we were a mixture of Spanish, black and white parents who got along well." She spoke of the "pleasure of being with kids and watching them have a good time without getting into trouble," and complimented the leadership of the two teachers and the school principal, Dr. Geren. "It was evident that as a student at Garden Hills you would be taught to respect the dignity and rights of your fellow students and their property."

Other school activities that depend heavily on volunteers are special dinners, award banquets, coffees and teas, where extra hands are needed to plan, coordinate, prepare and serve food; and, of course, to help put everything back in place when guests have left.

The annual international dinner at Garden Hills is very popular, requiring three to four months of planning. A parent who co-chaired the dinner one year regarded her participation in the dinner a rare opportunity to sample the many unusual foods prepared by parents and others, and to meet people representing a kaleidoscope of ethnic and international cultures. "Most of the food for our 300 some guests was brought to the cafeteria by parents," she said. My job was to secure volunteers and help from some of the restaurants in the community."

Garden Hills considers exposure to the cultural arts, at a very young age, an important adjunct to a well-rounded education. Its annual Young Audiences program embraces two off-campus events (such as concerts, ballets, etc.) and three in-school programs. This activity involves cooperation between the PTA, a teacher/sponsor and a volunteer parent. Sponsor and parent attend Young Audience previews and make program recommendations to the school staff and parents. In the main, the volunteer parent is in charge of collecting money — about $5 or $6 for each student. When it is known, generally by teachers, that a youngster's parents cannot afford the expense, the PTA picks up the tab. Young Audience artists come to the school to perform or have older students attend off-campus entertainment. Sometimes, however, Garden Hills students create and perform their own programs.

Dramatic and musical presentations by students provide more than entertainment for students and parents. They also spin off a multitude of educational benefits. But their preparation takes a lot of time — time not readily available to staff members. Fortunately, however, there are citizens who derive pleasure from working in a theatrical atmosphere. "It was fun," a former Twin Peaks officer said, "We helped the drama teacher set up competitions for students who wanted to put on an act. We judged all of the acts and then coordinated the final program for presentation to the public."

In an entirely different vein, a Rancho Bernardo attorney addressed a class at Twin Peaks on the subject of law in America. I asked him if he thought the students profited from his discussion of American jurisprudence and our system of constitutional law. He nodded. "I think so. I was rather shocked, though, to learn that they had no concept of the presumption of innocence, of the idea of due process. Merely reading about it in a textbook doesn't seem to take hold. The kids who are coming up today are going to be the jurors of tomorrow. If they're not taught the really important things, they are not going to be ready for their adult responsibilities. I remember that when I went to school I learned about an isosceles triangle — that the sum of the squares of the two sides equals the square of the hypotenuse. Now that was very interesting, but I have never had occasion to use that information."

Citing the system's failure to teach students how contracts work, about the rights of citizens, about marriage and divorce and dying and what to do if they lose their jobs and how to balance a checkbook, the attorney added, "And then when they get into trouble because they don't know any better, we wring our hands."

Another professional, a physician who had been working with Poway High School since 1979, told of his concern for the physical well-being of youngsters in interschool sports. He was particularly concerned about orthopedic and injury problems related to particular sports. "At first I tried to do mass screenings alone — maybe 100 to 150 over two or three nights. But I soon realized that the need was greater than I could provide, so I asked a physical therapist and a local orthopedist if they would volunteer their time along with me. The relationship with the young athletes is unique and something we all enjoy."

Community clubs provide incentives and support for school activities as demonstrated by the Twin Peaks area's Soroptimist Club whose membership includes the school principal and a counselor. With the help of club members and girls from the school, proceeds from a dance promoted by the group recently raised about $400 which was donated to an orphanage in Mexico. The students also collected, washed, folded and delivered an assortment of used clothing to the orphanage. In this instance, people who needed help were the beneficiaries of not one but two sources of volunteerism: adult members of the community and Twin Peaks students.

Boosters Club parents at McCluer North encourage and work closely with their children toward school goals. One of the school's biggest parent activity organizations, "Boosters" is credited with raising the needed $10,000 to help equip the weightlifting room, but members state their club's objectives go beyond fundraising: "We think it is important to recognize outstanding students for their academic as well as athletic achievements."

Working with foreign language teachers, parents support the high school's Student Exchange Program, through an annual exhibition and sale, in which USA families host students from other countries for a semester or a year and USA students go to foreign countries in exchange.

Project Graduation, McCluer North's big 1986-1987 PTSA undertaking, demonstrates how positive things can happen when parents, teachers and students work together to accomplish a specific goal. In this case the objective was to plan, synchronize and supervise an all-night, alcohol/ drug-free senior celebration — a night graduates would long remember with pleasure and pride. After 6:30 p.m., following the official graduation ceremonies, time was allotted for students to be with parents, friends and relatives.

Later that night, students converged on the North County YMCA which had been rented for the 24-hour Project Graduation festivities. What followed could never have happened without the enthusiastic boost and backing of a myriad of people who believed that it ought to be possible to celebrate one of life's most important occasions with a minimum of mishap.

Graduates met back at the school around 10:30 p.m. and rode the school buses to the Y. They had to have tickets to get in, and they had to stay until the next morning. "Basically, we locked them in," a parent explained. "We had security people there just to make sure that outsiders didn't come in or that students didn't sneak out."

There was something for everyone: dancing, casino games such as roulette and black jack (using play money), even swimming, handball, and racquetball for those so inclined. Long before graduation day, volunteers had so succesfully solicited the business community for door prizes that virtually every student at the party ended up with a souvenir. Throughout the night adult volunteers went out and brought in refreshments that were donated non-stop by a local pizza parlor.

Credit for the success of this unique graduation celebration was attributed almost entirely to the efforts and energies of volunteering parents. Teachers also joined in — sometimes as chaperones, but more often as participants in the fun. "Some teachers got together and played the seniors in a four-man volleyball game," one teacher commented, "but I don't remember who won. I do remember, though, that everyone had a good time."

At Garden Hills, a group numbering about twenty (consisting of outgoing PTA board members from the school year just ending, incoming board members, committee heads, teacher representatives and the school principal) attend the annual PTA retreat held at a mountain resort about sixty miles outside Atlanta. Here they set goals for the coming year, plan how to achieve them and discuss previous successes and failures. People who attend are considered the backbone of the PTA, and they generally agree that being together for a weekend of fun and work develops the kind of bond needed to sustain them through the tough times they may have to face during the coming school year.

Tackled topics range from studying how library volunteers can be more helpful to the school librarian to how the weekly newsletter put out by the 5th grade teacher and her students can be accomplished more efficiently.

"We talk a lot about fundraisers — a constant PTA problem," a participant explained. "And the international dance program, of which we are very proud, takes a lot of planning because of budgetary considerations and possible personnel changes. One of our most recent innovations is that a PTA officer will now go to faculty meetings. It has always been considered important for teachers to be represented at PTA board meetings so teachers will know what parents are thinking. Now, with someone from PTA in attendance at faculty meetings, parents will have a better opportunity to understand teachers' viewpoints."

Other questions I sought answers to at Garden Hills were how can the PTA stimulate community involvement when so many parents live a considerable distance from the school and when there are so many nationalities represented in the student body. One answer came in the form of an amazing recounting of how this school's PTA and faculty joined with area residents to combat a proposed urban renewal project. To the families involved, the buildings in jeopardy were their homes. In addition, as a result of relocation, their children would not be able to continue to attend Garden Hills.

In protest, one of the residents, an English-speaking American, organized her foreign-speaking neighbors — a move that drew the attention and support of the Garden Hills faculty and its principal who in turn mobilized the school's PTA. Together they incorporated a non-profit group known as SINA (Save International Neighborhoods in Atlanta), which raised several thousand dollars in legal fees in an attempt to halt the demolition.

Because of the publicity generated, the city's mayor soon became involved. Weekly SINA meetings were held in the school library, bringing together people of varied backgrounds with one purpose: to preserve an endangered neighborhood and its valued school whose enrollment would be drastically affected by a reduction in area residents. The battle that began near the end of one year continued well into spring.

It would be nice to report that the guys in the white hats won and the project went down in defeat, but it didn't happen that way. The resulting compromise, however, was far more palatable than the original threat.

Pressured by the public in general and school supporters in particular, developers agreed to leave standing 90 apartments which would be made available first to families with children of school age who would otherwise have to be moved to another district. Furthermore, any of the ninety apartments not occupied by such families would be offered next to the elderly and to those for whom moving would be most traumatic.

Other major undertakings by committed parents and community leaders illustrate the value of their influence in school-related matters. Mrs. Terri Milkey, 1983-1984 president of Garden Hills PTA, described how she, other parents and principal Dr. Geren counteracted the growing trend of area parents to enroll their children in private schools rather than placing them at Garden Hills. Contacts were made with numerous real estate agents who were selling homes in the Garden Hills district, inviting them to visit the school. They were obviously impressed with what they saw, for gradually they began to pass the word on to prospective buyers that living in the Garden Hills area had special merit: Their children would attend an outstanding school with a unique international appeal. The strategy paid off.

The School Site Council at Twin Peaks is a working forum for thinking through school improvement proposals and for making recommendations. Consisting of parent representatives from each of the state or federally funded programs (such as Gifted and Talented Education — GATE —), other parents, staff members and students, it is highly valued as an opportunity to actively participate in matters of importance. At these meetings, Council members feel free to discuss questionable school practices and often come away with the reassurance that efforts will be made to correct them.

"The administration might not always agree with you," one member said, "but they always bend over backwards to try to understand and accept different points of view."

A former chairman of the School Site Council recalled that after he raised questions about overcrowding in his son's algebra class, it wasn't long before Principal Judy Endeman found a way to provide an extra math section, a full-time teacher for the period and a second room for an additional class.

"Another time," the Council member continued, "I was shocked to discover from a writing assignment my son had asked me to proofread that it only contained one complete sentence! I brought the matter up with his basic ed teacher and the principal, neither of whom became defensive. They agreed that I had every right to be concerned. The teacher admitted that he did not know how to teach writing, and the principal immediately referred him to a writing course offered by the school district. Now, the entire school system has introduced a program that teaches teachers how to teach writing!"

Overcrowding at Garden Hills in English as a Second Language was also prevalent, particularly in 1983 when its teacher desperately needed help due to the ESL population boom. Pressures exerted by concerned parents and other citizens had a profound effect, for their open letter to the Board of Education resulted in the immediate hiring of a second ESL teacher. Some people responsible for initiating the action conceded that although they didn't enjoy these kinds of arm-twisting jobs, someone had to do them. Sometimes the principal's hands are tied, they say, but lay people can step in — and should — when they can do something valuable for their schools.

McCluer North's counterpart of Twin Peaks' School Site Council, which also involves active faculty and voluntary parent participation, is the principal's advisory committee. At the beginning of each school year, the first parent newsletter announces the advisory committee's initial meeting and invites everyone to attend. Advisors pass the word along to parents at open house meetings and other gatherings that if they would like to become better acquainted with their school, membership on the advisory committee is one of the best ways to do this. Monthly meetings seek to answer questions such as, Is the advisement system working? How can we improve parent-school communications? Is the program planning process clear? Is it well organized?

A parent who had served on the high school's advisory committee agreed that "to make public education first-class, parents have the responsibility to know what's going on in their schools. This doesn't mean that as volunteers our job is to look over the shoulders of the professionals, but it does let them know they have parental support and that the community is genuinely interested in what's going on in those classrooms."

Today at McCluer North the principal's advisory committee has been supplemented by the addition of the newly organized PTSA, a step many believe will further enhance the effectiveness of parent/teacher/student relationships.

Because of its location, size, grade levels and other variances, structure of volunteer activities at the Garden Hills Elementary school in Atlanta, Georgia, differs considerably from those at Twin Peaks in California or McCluer North in Missouri. But here, too, through organized group undertakings, parents exercise their "collective power." Here, too, parents complained that the pupil-teacher ratio was too high and that classroom teachers were obviously overworked. "Some of them didn't even have time to go to the bathroom," a parent noted. "Classroom teachers taught their own physical ed and art. Some of us parents joined together with NAPPS and sometimes APPLE Corps to see what could be done. There is now a full-time physical ed teacher and teacher aides in rooms where they are most needed."

At McCluer North High, a district-wide citizens' committee was named to survey school facilities and to decide what should be done about reduced enrollment. Principal Bill Hampton and assistant superintendent Arnold Potts served as non-voting members. There were no school board members on the committee. The committee concluded that a number of grade schools should be closed and that the district ought to consider the consolidation of two of the three high schools and the relocation to a third and neutral site. Although there was opposition to some of the committee's proposals, their report was ultimately adopted and some schools were closed.

A Ferguson-Florissant parent who served on the steering committee of McCluer North's 1986-1987 Strategic Planning Commission explained that their job was to plan for the district's next three to five years. The committee consisted of administrators, parents, teachers, principals and community members who were not parents. Twelve areas of concern were identified. Students were invited to express in subcommittees what they felt the district needed to do to improve student achievement, district standards in electronics, computers student self-esteem and community relations.

One of the goals of the steering committee was to plan how to change student attitudes from the temptation to 'just get by' to 'work to full capacity.' "It was gruelling," a participating parent said. "Sometimes we worked from eight in the morning until ten in the evening for two and three days straight. At first I told myself there was no way this was going to work, but as we continued, I became convinced that we would succeed, and we did."

125

While volunteers generally agree that the purpose of their participation is to fill school needs, they also testify to the satisfaction they personally derive from donating their time and efforts. "One of the things I was especially proud to have had a part in," a volunteer told me, "was the formation of a telephone committee to call parents and registered voters in the area to get their opinions on school matters." She also spoke of the many things she learned in her association with the school. She learned, for instance, that teachers and principals don't make all the rules — that many rules, if not most, come from the school board, and what volunteers try to do is important to the entire community. As a parent who was in business for herself, this volunteer paid particular attention to financial matters because she knew the importance of knowing where the money would come from to pay for new ideas or projects.

She stated further that the volunteers at her school did not feel their input was ignored. "Just the other day," she said, "the president of the board of education said to me, 'I don't want you to think we're not serious about your committee's recommendations.' " Then he told me how many hundreds of thousands of dollars the school would request to begin implementing the programs we had suggested."

Involvement of school volunteers sometimes extends from the classroom to the district and on to the state, as attested by Mary Faulk who described some of her experiences as chairperson of the Cooperating School Districts' legislative committee of St. Louis County. At the time, many of the states decided to get on the "improve education" bandwagon, and Missouri was one of them. A teacher of many years, Mrs. Faulk believed that state legislators did not do sufficient homework before plunging in and trying to force every school district in Missouri to conform to a single mold. She referred to their efforts as "legislating mediocrity." Legislators did not study current funding, she added, and subsequently discovered that their proposals would cost much more money than the state was willing to pay.

"Their pet project was a testing package for all schools that consisted of a state written criterion reference test," Mrs. Faulk related. "In our school district we had worked very hard developing our own curriculum and using our own tests to measure student success rates. We were an integrated community. We needed to consider unique community patterns. Because of our large size and because we have so many different socio-economic groups, we have to treat each one separately. Now the state was going to try to force us to change the way we met these challenges by insisting on the use of their testing criteria."

However, Mrs. Faulk's legislative committee was successful in influencing the state legislature to soften its stand. Schools would be permitted to use either the state written test, if they had no testing program of their own, or they could use their own test, if it met legislative guidelines. In

126

other words, the door was left open, allowing a school district to continue to run according to its individual needs.

Mrs. Faulk agreed that there were many good ideas in the state's proposals, but her main concern was where the money would come from. She cited that her school district operated predominantly on property tax revenues, that there was no room for growth — they were property bound. There was no easy way to raise taxes, either. To make matters worse, the district was experiencing a declining enrollment along with an expanding elderly population. "I hated to see carrots dangled before us and then fail to see the necessary money show up," Mrs. Faulk said. "What our committee, consisting of educators and lay people, accomplished was worth the hard work."

Forty-five years ago a few small suburban districts in St. Louis County worked together to strengthen their educational programs. Rather than weakening during critical changing times, the group grew stronger. The Great Depression, World War II, Sputnik, and other social and educational developments stimulated rather than stifled its effectiveness. Cooperating School Districts now number 44 and include not only the 24 districts in St. Louis County but also 20 districts in three adjoining counties.

Warren Brown, superintendent of the Ferguson-Florissant school district several years before McCluer North became a school, and for several years after it opened, praised the atmosphere of support and cooperation among the school districts and school boards in this organization. "The Cooperating School Districts organization was primarily responsible for most of the educational progress made in Missouri. It had an on-going lobbying organization that worked for better financing of schools; it encouraged financing of special projects such as early childhood centers and smaller class sizes. It was an instrument of innovation."

"That's well and good," I agreed, "but where did the money come from?"

Mr. Brown answered, "The state aid for education increased at least 100 percent during the period I was working in Missouri. The state finally developed a program that was based on the local district's wealth. Those with less resources got more money, and those that were wealthier got less."

Admittedly, the degree to which funds and other resources are made available, the quantity and quality of regulations which must be followed, and the imposition of a variety of restrictions — all exert tremendous influences on local school districts. But parents and community leaders also can exercise considerable control over those who, through the political power vested in them, make the rules, enact the laws, and mete out the money.

In an earlier chapter, Twin Peaks Middle School's "Safari to Sacramento" was discussed. Much pre-planning went into this major undertaking to sway legislative decisions regarding California's now nationally-famous Proposition 13. First, legislators in metropolitan San Diego were in-

127

vited to Twin Peaks for a day. Four legislators came and three others were represented by their assistants. After spending considerable time in classrooms where students surprised everyone with their knowledge, wit and ease in asking and answering questions of the visitors, open house was held in a nearby school facility. Three hundred and fifty people from the city of Poway just "roamed in," not all of whom had young people at Twin Peaks. Feedback from this open meeting reported that "there were some very hot and heavy questions asked which were totally unrelated to education. So the legislators who attended the open house were impressed."

Teachers of the basic education classes which the legislators had visited reported that the occasion "brought reality into the classes — truly a high point in the education of students who participated in the discussions." Legislative Day also prepared the way for the "safari" to the capital, a "junket" that undeniably had an impact on the passage of legislation related to the state's schools.

Many of the volunteers I interviewed did not have children in the schools they assisted, but considered their donation of time a matter of community responsibility. And they all had interesting stories to tell about how they first became involved in school activities — some benefited from encouragement and moral support of "veteran" volunteers while others had to "learn the ropes" on their own. More than once reference was made to the National School Volunteer Program, Inc., as an excellent source of information on the subject of school volunteerism. This national non-profit education association is credited with directly influencing the quality of volunteer training in one-fourth of the 16,000 school districts across the country. Citizens who want to take a more active role in their schools might want to begin by writing to NSVP, Inc.; Suite 320; 701 N. Fairfax Street; Alexandria, Virginia 22314.

A veteran volunteer offers additional advice to potential volunteers:

. . . Talk with other parents about what is going on in the school.

. . . Talk to the principal and teachers.

. . . Attend any meetings of parents or other groups at the school; observe what is happening, what is not happening.

. . . Make inquiries about whether or not the school has a School Improvement Program and if it has an operating School Site Council.

. . . Ask if there is a private foundation that supports the school.

Does the school have a parent club or PTSA? What kind of support is the school utilizing to build its programs? Take a look at other potential community resources. Find out what other schools in the district are doing. If what you see and hear uncovers areas of need, go to the principal and say, "I would like to help make such-and-such happen. Would you help me get it started?" Or "Can you direct me to a group of volunteers or someone in the district who is willing to work with me to see that such-and-such gets started?"

Citizens who are willing to take these first steps soon become working partners with their schools and experience great satisfaction in their successful accomplishments. Mrs. Terry Fischer, prominent St. Louis civic leader who has devoted numerous years of service to education advises that for our democratic society to function on course, efforts of individual lay people to take the initiative in school matters are not only desirable, but indispensable. She also believes there are two essential ingredients for success: One is the willingness of individuals to take the initiative and the other is timing. But, she warns, one has to be prepared for a slow measure of progress.

"There is a definite place for the lay person in our schools," Mrs. Fischer said, "and an opportunity to make a positive contribution to the improvement of education in our country. It takes time, study, persistence, hard work, joining hands with professional educators, working together and yes, we mustn't forget, a good measure of political savvy." To honor Mrs. Fischer's untiring service to the community, one of the buildings at the St. Louis Community College in Florissant Valley is named the Terry Fischer Theater.

My four years as coordinator of the Grandpeople Program in the Poway District, plus my experiences as a teacher, principal and superintendent provide personal insights into the subject of volunteerism in our schools. At Twin Peaks, "freewill workers" are recruited by the coordinator of the Grandpeople Program. Two-thirds of the coordinator's time on the job is donated; the other third is compensated by the school at a modest hourly rate. It should be noted too, that the local Kiwanis Club included the Grandpeople Program in their 1986-1987 budget with a contribution of more than $1,000.

I found community group meetings a rich opportunity for making contacts. At the beginning of each gathering, it took but a few moments to collect names and telephone numbers of people who thought they might be interested in helping out at the school. When I asked volunteers how they felt about their contributions, their reactions were varied:

"You just can't go to PTA and hug your administrator, buy her a corsage, and think you are going to make a difference. What makes the difference is perspiration and participation."

"A parent should be sure to volunteer to do something even if it's nothing more than bringing refreshments to class on a holiday or someone's birthday."

"If there's no set volunteer program in your school and you're shy about going directly to the principal, you could start by calling the principal's secretary. Just say whatever's on your mind. So many people say to me, 'How come you know all this? It would have saved me a lot of heartache if I'd known.' All you have to do is ask."

"Even if it's uncomfortable, force yourself. Don't be like a lot of people who don't even know where the principal's office is. Some don't even know where the nurse's door is. If your school doesn't have an open door policy, as Twin Peaks does, ask if you can be the person who opens it. It won't be long before you're showing around ten other parents so they can become a part of the school, too.''

"I'm constantly amazed at how some parents think they can cope with their children, from grade school through high school, without taking an active part in what's going on.''

The number of families in which both parents work the five days a week that schools are in session reaches fifty percent in many communities, and sometimes more. How to establish a working relationship with these kinds of homes takes special skills, plus a willingness to go beyond customary practices. At Twin Peaks, for instance, the principal stood fast in her determination to have evening coffees in the neighborhoods where most families worked, and although they were scheduled to last only one hour, they often exceeded two. A lot of territory can be covered in two hours. These meetings have proven a golden opportunity for working parents to have their questions answered by both the principal and faculty members in attendance. They also help to establish contacts which simplify future lines of communication.

The advisory system at McCluer North depends heavily on telephone contacts, evenings or on weekends, between working parents and advisors. In addition to telephone contacts, however, it is not unusual for working parents to find additional time to become actively involved in school matters as follows:

Monitor a school board meeting as a representative of the PTSA. This simply requires someone to sit in on the meetings, observe the proceedings, record what actually transpired, including perhaps some personal reactions and conclusions about the roles parents can take in strengthening school or district levels, and presenting a written report to the PTSA board.

Organize "meet-your-candidate" evenings at board election time during which candidates state positions and answer questions; and/or present to would-be voters an analysis by neutral observers of past effectiveness of board members seeking re-election.

Learn as much as possible about the people who are running for or are elected to public offices. Volunteers with this knowledge (previously referred to by a volunteer as "political savvy") often become indispensable links between legislators and citizens when parent groups want to be heard.

Help teachers and interested lay people keep up to date about national news concerning our schools. Today there is much information proliferated on the subject of education, but teachers don't ordinarily find the extra time needed to keep abreast of current research and trends. Nonetheless, if they are to be their most effective, they need the information. I speak from personal experience that teachers appreciate finding in their mail boxes copies of material that one day might have a bearing on their work.

130

For the most part, parents regard their active and visible participation in school matters at the elementary level not only acceptable but essential. As their youngsters advance through middle and high schools, however, many parents begin to view their continued personal involvement differently. They begin to feel intrusive, unwanted, unnecessary. But when I asked a volunteer, "Do your high-schoolers resent your involvement in their school activities?" she said, "Not at all — my kids think it's great. And if the truth were known, we'd find that adolescents prefer to have their parents involved. While we know this to be true in sports, it also shows up in other areas. True, kids don't come out and admit it up front, so it's best to play it cool — you have to give them some space. But no matter how we do it, we mustn't let our involvement go down as the ages of our children go up."

Another parent told me she always regretted not becoming a working partner at Twin Peaks until her son was in the 7th grade. She let other parents convince her that kids didn't want their parents around — "they don't need you," they said. "But I discovered for myself that they did want me and they did need me. Before I became directly involved, I didn't know the kids my son talked about at home. I really wanted to get to know them and to be able to set some direction in my son's life. I have never regretted taking the initiative. By the time my younger daughter came along behind her brother in school, I was right in the thick of things. I felt comfortable going to a teacher or to the principal and saying 'Wasn't that great?' or 'I have a question,' or 'I have a complaint.' "

When one student learned that her mother was considering attending school on Shadow Day, her unconcealed discomfort almost convinced her mother not to go. But, over her daughter's protests, the mother appeared in her daughter's classes anyway. "I enjoyed visiting her classes very much," she told me. "Later my daughter apologized for wishing I wouldn't attend. Now she says she's glad I know so much about her program at school. I also know that my visit opened up new channels of communication between the two of us."

What do you do when your school gives you the message that it doesn't want your help? When I asked that question of an Atlanta citizen widely recognized and acknowledged as an expert in educational matters, he first reminded me of the new age in which we are living — one in which family life is very different from earlier times. Part of this difference he accurately attributed to three factors: our rapid technological growth, the great number of homes in which both parents now work, and the fact that a large percentage of our schools are multi-ethnic in makeup. "In spite of these dramatic changes, we still expect our schools to take our children just as they are and do well by them," he said. "The very least we can do is to help our schools wherever we think we can do the most good."

Then, in answer to my question, he described how one PTA, consisting of only fourteen members (7% of its potential), was able to chip away at its school's indifference to volunteers. Inasmuch as the school was a designated election polling place, the PTA sponsored a project in which visitors were welcomed as they entered the school to vote. During the long election day, coffee was served, and staff members frequently stopped by, encouraging conversation between PTA members, residents and staff.

Another time, a tax rate election was forthcoming which, if successful, would increase the school district's budget. The PTA volunteered to sponsor a meeting so parents, residents and staff members could assemble and become better informed about suggested changes before going to the polls. Needless to say, the school staff deeply appreciated the efforts of this PTA which accomplished its intended goal.

The same PTA, providing both transportation and adult supervision, also sponsored a field trip for pupils to visit the local library to find out how it is financed. School people accepted this approach to learning about the local use of monies for civic purposes and gave the parents' group its blessing and cooperation.

One project led to another: PTA invited local bank personnel to stop at the school on their way to work to help students learn more about money, how to budget it and how to spend it; PTA members secured volunteers to offer before-school classes for students interested in learning a second language; PTA cooperated with the staff in putting on a carnival for the school's 190 students.

A Garden Hills volunteer provides this advice to citizens who want to help their schools but don't know where to begin: "Avoid pressuring. Don't push your way in. Rather, find the school's most pressing needs and figure out a way to try to help the staff meet those needs."

The Twin Peaks volunteer program consists of two branches. The first includes the principal and the PTSA board. The second, named the Grandpeople Program, is headed up by an appointed coordinator and consists of citizens who want to contribute to a particular project, such as helping in the classrooms, describing memorable experiences or participating in the Mystery Guest program. This program, providing 6th graders with an introduction to vocations, had 35 guests during one year, each of whom met with four separate classes.

The Grandpeople Program had its start at Westwood Elementary School in the Poway District in 1982. After several unsuccessful attempts by the school's principal, Bill Banner, to attract volunteers by placing posters in stores and announcements in newspapers, he decided as a last resort to hire a half-time coordinator, an idea that worked.

Twin Peaks Principal Judy Endeman agreed that Banner's plan was a good one, and, in spite of the opposition of those who felt that while it may be appropriate at the elementary level it could not possibly succeed in a middle school, Mrs. Endeman elected to try it. The program also succeeded in meeting the volunteer needs of the middle school.

Ken Swanson, current coordinator of the Twin Peaks Grandpeople Program, talked about his job. "I appeal primarily to senior citizens to help the school by spending one or two hours a week, generally on a one-to-one basis with students. I view my role as one of channeling communication between the school's requirements and potential volunteers. Success as a coordinator, I think, depends on an understanding of individual teacher requirements and the volunteers' interests, experiences and abilities. Job satisfaction for everyone concerned results from a good 'fit' wherein the teacher, the volunteer, and the student end up happy with the assignment. During the course of my work, I'm often reminded of one of Winston Churchill's quotations: 'We make a living by what we get. We make a life by what we give.' "

Letters, listing specific areas in which the school could use help, are sent to parents at the beginning of the school year. "We don't just call a parent or ask on a written form 'Do you want to help at school?' " explained one parent volunteer. "We let them know exactly what we need. There are so many people who have special talents and interests. If anything on our list appeals to them, they will immediately pick up on it because they know it's something 'right down their alley.' "

Sometimes principals or PTSA leaders becomes so excited about the possibilities of certain programs that they decide to take shortcuts to develop them. I have learned that nothing can kill a volunteer program faster than putting it prematurely into high gear. It should be allowed to grow as it merits growth, a measurement dependent on its degree of success.

This became clearer to me as I worked on the Grandpeople Program. A teacher knew what he was talking about when he told me, "I don't want to take on a volunteer yet. Too many new ideas fall by the wayside too quickly. I'm going to wait and see if this idea takes root." Six months later he asked for, and got, one volunteer. Three years later he had three.

Kicking off a volunteer program is the easy part. Keeping it alive and well is the hard part and requires constant nurturing. At Twin Peaks, fall and spring appreciation luncheons honor its volunteers, with teachers and students assisting in preparation and serving. In addition, each year PTSA leadership sponsors a luncheon or tea which also expresses its appreciation to the staff, to those in the Grandpeople Program and to all other participating volunteers. Still another way the school has of saying thank you is through an after-school computer class offered especially for Grandpeople volunteers.

At the elementary school level, Principal Peggy Geren invites staff, volunteers and parent leaders to her home for dinner in an informal setting. This demonstration of appreciation is not wasted. Everyone benefits from the time spent together and comes away with a renewed spirit that his or her contributions have been valuable and recognized.

Enthusiasm for the advisory program at McCluer North appears to be contagious enough to sustain that program without the need for much additional encouragement. As staunch supporters of the system, advisors work very hard to develop good relationships with each parent — an effort that obviously pays off. Parents are made to feel that they are a necessary part of their youngsters' educational process and show their appreciation by cooperating wherever possible.

Although Garden Hills and Twin Peaks do not rely on a formal advisory program (as does McCluer North) to bridge the communication gap between staff, students and parents, they have created their own methods for accomplishing the same objectives. What works in one school does not necessarily mean it will work in another. Each of the three schools, however, has excelled as the result of the extra dimension provided by their voluntary partners. It is hard for me to conceive any school becoming "excellent" without on-going help from the community.

CHAPTER SIX

Seven Common Characteristics of Good Schools and How to Attain Them
by Deede Sharpe

Four chapters in this book detail both the outcomes and the sources of educational excellence in three schools. In reading these accounts, I am struck with similarities between these schools and numerous excellent companies I have studied. As former manager of educational program development for the Walt Disney World Co., I remain overwhelmed at the number of image-building techniques employed by the Disney organization that could successfully be applied in our schools. And, since leaving Walt Disney World Co., I have researched a number of other strong companies whose records are impressive and whose employees are happy, and found many of the same "Disney" practices in place.

Any service industry achieves its goals through people, and the basic human principles that motivate people toward excellent performance are universal. Whether it is the smile that tells consumers they are special, the up-to-date answers for consumers' questions, or providing above-average service to meet consumers' needs, all successful organizations have descriptors of excellence and related causes behind those indicators.

There seems to be a common set of strategies (which might be labeled strategies of "people management") that produce success in industry. Such strategies can be adapted by any organization in any environment. The three schools described in this book rely on these same strategies. What follows is a capsule of seven principles behind the strategies, which can serve two purposes:

1. As a summary of the elements behind the excellence of these three schools, and

2. As a checklist by which to steer your own plans for improvement of your school's or organization's climate for achievement.

135

IN EVERY EFFECTIVE SCHOOL, THE CLIMATE IS POSITIVE, PROMOTING A DESIRE TO CARE.

Bad News: You cannot make people care. You cannot train people to care. You cannot even fire people who do not care. Care is a personal, human emotion that comes from within.

Good News: You can create a climate in which people want to care, in which people exert extra effort, take extra time, take pride in their work and their association with the organization.

All three of these schools can be characterized as having that positive climate in which people want to care. Upon entering the buildings, visitors almost immediately sense that "good things are happening here." Most experienced school people know that the reverse is also true — negative images conveyed to visitors do affect everyone else in the environment.

In every organization, the climate is established and readily observable. Questions are: How is the climate controlled? How do you produce a positive climate? Some of the answers can be found in the descriptions of Garden Hills, Twin Peaks, and McCluer North schools.

IN EVERY EFFECTIVE SCHOOL, THERE EXISTS A CLEAR ORGANIZATIONAL PERSONALITY, CHARACTERIZED BY STATED MISSIONS, GOALS, VALUES AND STANDARDS OF PERFORMANCE.

Alice: "Would you please tell me which way I ought to go from here?"
Cheshire Cat: "Well, that depends a good deal on where you want to go."
Alice: "I don't much care where."
Cheshire Cat: "Then it doesn't much matter which way you go."

Lewis Carroll
Alice in Wonderland

"Who are you?"
"Where have you been?"
"Where are you going?"
"What have you to declare?"
Canadian Customs Agent
Vancouver, B. C., Canada

Organizations, like individuals, are much happier, healthier and better directed, if they can answer the Cheshire Cat and the Customs Agent. These three schools have in common the basics in structuring a positive climate for achievement. They have established clear goals, a sense of mission, standards . . . an organizational personality that everyone in the organization can "buy into." And the life expectancy of that model personality can be extended greatly by committing the group's mission and stan-

136

dards to writing; and by highlighting them in everything the organization does or produces.

The second critical climate element — involvement — is illustrated by how the personality was structured in the first place: Goals, mission, and values were not determined by an administrative committee — they were the products of everyone's thinking, everyone involved with the school.

IN EVERY EFFECTIVE SCHOOL, PEOPLE ARE INVOLVED — ALL THE PEOPLE, ALL THE TIME.

As basic as the principle of involvement is, one wonders at its lack of universal application; especially since schools, service industries, manufacturing concerns, civic organizations and even homes that practice involvement in decision making are often highlighted as exceptional and successful. One reason why involvement seems to be a rare management practice may well be the lack of positive role models. Many executives, who were themselves managed autocratically, have difficulty visualizing how involvement might happen. Garden Hills, Twin Peaks and McCluer North address this shortage of examples.

Exemplified by Twin Peaks' School Site Council, involvement was first sought on what the mission and values of the school ought to be, and involvement continues through the constant up-dating of stated goals and programs. If a clear mission statement and widely accepted goals are characteristic of a positive climate, and if involvement in the achievement of those goals is a value, then the logical place to start getting people involved is in the goal-setting process. People involved in identifying the goals work much harder to help accomplish them. By starting their goal-setting task with a questionnaire to parents, Twin Peaks raised the base of parental awareness upon which the goal-setting process could be productive. Too often, involvement is attempted at a decision-making level before those to be involved are even aware of the need.

Another characteristic evidenced in all three schools is everyone's *continued* involvement. Involvement is not an item to be checked off the list for the visiting school accreditation team. It is a way of managing the school. As McCluer North teachers noted, their "advisory teams are an integral part of the school." Involvement applies not only to festivals and career exploration; it is a way of doing business. Every decision is made with input from those to be affected by the decision. The school would not consider operating in isolation. Parents, students and the community are truly partners in the educational enterprise.

A third common denominator of successful involvement found at the schools is the high value placed on listening. Each school exhibits an openness, a receptivity to ideas from all quarters. From formal meetings to questionnaires to informal in-put, all three schools have mechanisms by

137

which to measure their audiences and encourage feedback, by listening to individuals, as well as "organization listening;" i.e., through polling, focus groups, and questionnaires.

This leads to the fourth characteristic of effective involvement evident at the three schools. The contributions people make are considered important and the contributors are rewarded and recognized — they see the pay-offs of their efforts.

Involvement is not an easy way to run a school. It demands planning, time and energy. However, it is the only way to run a school if the school is run for the educational benefit of students in a democratic society.

IN EVERY EFFECTIVE SCHOOL, PEOPLE ARE INFORMED . . . CONSTANT COMMUNICATIONS BETWEEN ADMINISTRATION, STAFF, PARENTS AND COMMUNITY ARE A GIVEN.

In any good organization, as demonstrated by the three schools, there is concern for "getting the news out." "How will this affect others, and how can I let them know?" seems to be the modus operandi.

Communication in any organization of more than, say, five individuals seems to be an ever present challenge. Employee opinion polls almost always show that communication needs improvement. Employees feel better the more they know, and they never think they know enough. So, these three schools, like other strong organizations, use as many channels of communication as often and as effectively as possible.

Effective schools do not rely on the printed word alone, nor do they communicate only through meetings. News is gathered constantly and disseminated through group meetings, as well as one-on-one contacts. News goes to the community through school newspapers, mass media, and a planned public relations program. There is a system, a structured process through which students, teachers and parents know they can express concerns and get responses. And the schools listen. They are in tune with their consumers, they have a planned system for gathering data, and they are dedicated to keeping their public informed.

THE EFFECTIVE SCHOOL DOESN'T JUST TAKE; IT GIVES, TOO. THE SCHOOL IS A CONTRIBUTORY PARTNER TO THE COMMUNITY IT SERVES.

The band director in the comic strip, "Funky Winkerbean," has become synonymous with the image some people have of the school's version of a partnership: "all take and no give." Indeed, school leaders, looking at all their needs and the abundance of resources in the community, rarely have the time to think through what the school can do for the community. These three schools are different.

From Garden Hills' activist role in APPLE and NAPPS, to McCluer North's providing speakers and facilities to local civic and cultural organizations, to a Twin Peaks student helping a Grandparent to his car, these schools give in return for their community support.

Schools that are one-way recipients of community support are, by their actions, exemplifying a "something-for-nothing" expectation. They set in motion, albeit unwittingly, the idea that "people will do things for me." Conversely, the schools highlighted here teach young people that they have a responsible part to play in society, that as youngsters or teenagers, their contributions are valued. It is interesting to watch adults who, after keeping young people in passive, non-contributing roles for eighteen years, are surprised when high school graduates feel no compunction to work or contribute anything to society. By contributing, students learn to contribute. By being responsible, students learn responsibility. By sharing in the work of the community, students gain a sense of community and belonging. By giving themselves to the community, teachers and students alike develop a sense of pride and self-worth.

Another point: These three schools are teaching tomorrow's volunteers today. By demonstrating civic responsibility, the schools demonstrate behaviors that, we hope, will be practiced by their students in the years ahead as they become adults, active in their own communities and in the support of their children's schools ten to twenty years hence.

THE EFFECTIVE SCHOOL FOLLOWS THE PRINCIPLE OF "DO AS I SAY *AND* AS I DO."

One has only to look at the grim statistics showing the majority of child abusers as, themselves, formerly abused children, to know the power of role-modeling as a teaching force. Earlier in this chapter, I hypothesized that the lack of participatory management may be due, in part, to the fact that today's managers were never involved, as workers, in decision making.

The power of role-modeling gives added importance to the roles principals, teachers and parents play in Garden Hills, Twin Peaks and McCluer North schools. The principals do not just tell teachers to be involved; the principals are involved with students and the community right alongside the teachers. The parents do not just say to students, "You can have fun without booze"; they are there, too, participating in the clean fun on graduation night. Administrators do not just tell teachers to listen to parents; the administrators actively seek parental input.

Nothing fosters the achievement of organizational goals more quickly than the active participation and role-modeling of those in charge. If it is important, then those in authority do it — they don't just talk about it. A critical success element runs throughout the three schools: Those in charge model behaviors that they say are important, that they want from teachers and students.

139

THE EFFECTIVE SCHOOL KNOWS WHERE IT IS AT ALL TIMES. IT KNOWS THE IMPORTANCE OF ASSESSMENT.

Ever play golf without keeping score? Not many golfers do. Consider how many fans would attend major league baseball or football if there were no points for runs or touchdowns. But many schools operate this way — running along, day in and day out, never assessing where they are in terms of the goals they once established as having high priority.

As important as goal-setting is, however, it is a waste of time and energy if performance is not continuously assessed in terms of the goals. Assessment of direction toward agreed upon goals provides schools with constant feedback on how well they are doing in terms of what they say they want to do.

Assessment at Garden Hills, Twin Peaks and McCluer North is on-going; and like their approach to communications discussed earlier, their assessment, too, keeps asking, "Where are we? What's going on here?"

Assessment is not limited to the standardized scores that are part of every educator's life. All in the organization have their "antennae" tuned to improvement. The goals are always the focus. "If these are our goals, how could we meet them more effectively?"

Walt Disney called it "plussing the show." He wanted Disney employees to be constantly on the look-out for anything that might improve the quality of the company's performance. This is the same broad interpretation of assessment carried out by the three schools. Note the following:

Curriculum: constantly reviewed.

Individual student progress: constantly discussed, with adjustments made mid-stream to address shortcomings.

Teacher performance: assessed routinely.

School's effectiveness: assessed by communities and students.

Constant assessment provides these three schools with marketing data to promote their accomplishments and to identify what needs fixing. Not infrequently, businesses that do not continually assess products and performance end up in the red. Similarly, schools for whom assessment is not a way of life often fall short of their goals, experience "teacher burn-out" and have a tough time exciting parental support. People like to support winners.

Constant comprehensive assessment of students, staff and curriculum makes teachers feel involved. It gives them personal responsibility for and pride in their achievements. It also lets parents and students know how excellent their school really is. You can't take pride in your team if you don't know the score.

Garden Hills, Twin Peaks, and McCluer North schools show what can be accomplished when communities and schools work together to create a positive climate for learning. Climate does not happen as a result of any ex-

140

ternal pressures or influences. Climate comes from the people involved. These people took charge of their climate. They determined what climate they wanted and then set the systems in place to produce that climate.

HOW CAN YOU BECOME INVOLVED?

Parents and Other Community Members

Schools need help on almost every level, from one-on-one involvement with students to legislative and policy support. What are your strengths and talents? How can you best help your schools?

First, consider your possible impact on educational policy in the district, state and nation. Education is a public service. Its success is in the hands of decision makers who determine funding and set directions. These decision makers are either supportive of schools and value the long-term contributions of education to a democracy; critical of schools and backing off of America's commitment to universal quality education; or somewhere in the uncommitted in-between. In any case, they are elected (or appointed by those elected), by people who do or do not vote.

The first level of involvement with schools begins by becoming an enlightened citizen. Learn about the candidates and their views on education. Support those who support schools *as a top priority* and make your findings known to those around you. Communicate your support to your preferred candidates and continue to express your views and concerns after election. Keep tabs on candidates' performance and communicate the record to others.

Learn about tax rates and bond issues and actively seek support for schools when local funding opportunities arise.

Become familiar with the data on how schools attract and keep businesses, and enhance property values in your area. Use this data to stimulate taxpayer support of education.

On the school level, much more than informed citizen support is needed. Schools need people to help teach; keep records; assist in student activities both on and off campus; coordinate and provide community-based learning opportunities for individuals and groups; spearhead publicity, public relations and miscellaneous communication efforts; as well as a host of other support functions.

Educators' professional hours are filled primarily with direct student contact. This often leaves undone a wide range of enrichment, community and tutorial tasks. Review your own interests, talents and experiences to determine where and how you might best contribute your services.

Your professional activities make you an expert in some areas, while your travel and other life experiences may qualify you as a cultural resource. Your hobbies and other leisure interests, from cooking to photography to computers, may be the content of a guest lecture or one-on-one tu-

141

toring. Or you may prefer to lend a hand in record-keeping, writing, coordinating or other non-student contact assignments. Almost any function that goes on in a service industry goes on in schools, and almost all schools could use extra help.

Take a personal inventory of your talents, interests and resources, and list services you might perform for your schools. The following is only a partial listing of how your skills could be used:

Tutoring, one-on-one with learners

Help in areas of your interest (i.e., art, foreign language, home economics, industrial arts, the school office)

Help teachers and administrators with paperwork

Assist clubs or athletic groups

Assist with field trips, social events

Coordinate community-based learning Help develop and implement a marketing plan to communicate the success of your school to the community

Recruit other individuals and organizations to become involved in their schools

Offer your business as an individual or group learning site for career education and vocational training

Being prepared in advance with specifics about what you can do (and when) will help your school's administrator communicate with teachers and make the most of your time and talents. Call ahead for an appointment with your principal, guidance counselor, volunteer coordinator or your child's teacher. Visit and volunteer. Your school needs you.

Educators

List all the functions in which parents and others could be, and should be, involved — from setting goals to participating in a structured public relations and marketing campaign. Discuss in staff meetings the benefits of, and barriers to, community involvement to the school, the learner and the individual educator. Devise options for overcoming barriers and create a plan for recruiting, using and recognizing community involvement. The plan should include activities through which the school will contribute to the community. If your school lacks a clear mission, goals and values, then the community involvement plan should start there, as it did at Twin Peaks.

Each school employee . . . teachers, administrators, secretaries, busdrivers — everyone . . . might answer questions like these:

1. What are your most critical needs with which the right person could help?
2. If you had a volunteer to help you tomorrow, what would you have them do?

3. What activities would be "nice to do" if you had the help to do them?
4. What services could you and the students provide back to the community?

The parent, civic organization, or interested citizen who calls to see how they might help the school is impressed with a knowledgeable, specific answer. A file of "job openings" for volunteers says the school is organized, needs and appreciates the contributions of the community. The "job openings" file is the base of a volunteer recruiting campaign.

Staff development sessions on effectively using and communicating with volunteers might be important if there seems to be hesitation from the staff. Schools have long been the private domain of educators. Most professionals on the job today were never taught, nor did they ever see, strong school-community partnerships. Open discussions, staff involvement in outlining the plans, and structured training sessions are effective in bridging the gap between the educator as boss and the educator as partner. The time spent getting everyone comfortable, as well as enthusiastic, about community involvement is critical. The ineffective use of volunteers can be counter-productive, resulting in negative public relations.

Parents and other community members have a vested interest in the success of schools. Each and every neighborhood is filled with people eager to share with others their skills, interests and talents. A viable school-community partnership increases the pool of available teachers and other learning resources, decreases discipline problems, improves student achievement and enhances community support for the professionalism of education. Perhaps no other single improvement effort can reap greater rewards. Garden Hills, Twin Peaks and McCluer North are the proof.

These schools "made good," and they did it through planning, productive classrooms and partnerships with their communities. In all these schools, there was no magic, no pixie dust — just caring, concerned people using basic principles of human behavior. People want to be involved, they want to know what's going on, they want to be associated with excellence, and they will work hard to make it happen — if you let them.